D0978298

The
Little Girl in the
Yellow Dress

A Musical Memoir Digging for the Roots of Performance Anxiety

Nancy Kaesler

Some names and identifying details have been changed
by the author to protect the privacy of individuals.

Copyright © 2014 Nancy Kaesler
All rights reserved.

ISBN: 1495488292
ISBN 13: 9781495488290
Library of Congress Control Number: 2014902947
CreateSpace Independent Publishing Platform
North Charleston, South Carolina

For Walt, first and always

and for the door openers

Dot Wheeler
Nettie Ruth Bratton
Jan Deats
William Westney

CONTENTS

Background

Skills and Blockages

Connecting Dots

Finding Answers

Perspective

Epilogue

ACKNOWLEDGMENTS

"YOU NEED TO write a book!" repeated by close friends often enough begins to be real, and you start to believe it. For this trust and encouragement, freely given, I am profoundly grateful to Sally Bonkrude, Catlyn Fendler, Mary Lampkin, Sara McDaniel, and William Westney.

In the earliest days of this process, they were of immeasurable help with concepts and editing—Catlyn with expert advice on writing, Sally and Mary with a vision of what the content could be, Sara with encouraging feedback from the Studio "trenches," and William with critical and professional expertise and support.

I want to say a resounding "Thank you!" for support in manuscript reading and the resulting helpful comments to Shana Kirk for her terrific suggestions about getting started and developing the content, to Kitty Keim, who has a sharp eye for errors both grammatical and typographical, to Nancy Breth for a closer look at the connections among ideas, and to Beth Klingenstein for good ideas about details and questions about meanings.

Jennifer Lukas made a wonderful contribution with her illustrations, Dawn Normali produced an inspired painting for the cover, and Donna Patterson consistently boosted my morale as a writer. I so appreciated my new friends in Trail Ridge Writers for their enthusiastic support and encouragement.

To my children and stepchildren goes deep appreciation for their consistent encouragement and loving support: David and Sam Allen, Judy Parker, Mike Kaesler, and Jan Gilbert.

Walt, my husband, has been patient and supportive, never faltering in his belief not only that I *could* write this book, but that I *needed* to. Thank you for being there all the way through the process.

PREFACE

IMAGINE TAKING A WALK through a garden, watching seeds planted long ago lie dormant, germinate, and break through soil to light. Life is often like that.

Looking back, I can see that each part of my own garden has developed in just the right way. Time has had little to do with it. It was only when I began active cultivation, asking questions and digging for answers, that things seemed to move toward flowering more insistently.

I have written about connecting the dots between my personal experience, as a student and a teacher of piano, and the larger context of music performance. The memoir describes my early training in piano, when seeds were sown. Along the way, while the buds of skills were being acquired, the weeds of intense anxiety about performance often blocked my success.

My search to understand this anxiety expanded, like cultivation of a garden. I asked many questions of old family letters and of books. I learned a great deal from other teachers and performers. I wanted to discover what had made me so afraid of playing before an audience when the thing I desired most was to share the music. What were the roots of my performance anxiety, and why had it caused such a struggle in my musical experience?

Would I teach my little-girl self differently today? In the first part of the book, I have interspersed my autobiographical narrative with comments from a teacher's point of view. These comments relate immediately to points in the story.

Continuing with reflections on my musical journey and on teaching, in the latter part of the book I have added a brief look at some elements of anxiety in general and in my family history in particular. I have followed a path that led to a look at the history of music performance. Has there always been a relationship between embedded anxiety and performance?

The taproot of music, its depth and meaning, is what we desire to communicate in performance. Exploring some examples of the evolution of the role of music performance in society has added to my perspective. Harvesting new insights from my "garden" helped me tie things together.

When I retired, I wanted to write about my experience. I was leaving a well-established, independent piano teaching studio and closing my workplace after forty-five years, but it wasn't as hard as I had feared. Moving away, but not too far away, kept me connected enough with my state organization of music teachers (of which I had been president for two years as well as a leader in other ways) to maintain collegial friendships and to teach by virtue of program presentation and adjudication commentaries.

I thoroughly enjoyed my long career. However, despite honors granted me and the treasured friendship of longtime colleagues and students, I always felt the desire to keep growing and offering more.

The deep pleasure of helping many students develop their technique, skills, and in some cases, profound and lasting musicality, was at once thrilling and humbling. Like a parent, perhaps, a teacher longs to provide the best possible experience for her students, offering some of the most precious moments of her own background while sparing everyone the most horrific—like *performance anxiety*, that deep anxiety associated with performing at the instrument—that aborted expression of the soul in music making.

I think that growing up in my studio was a positive experience for the vast majority of the students who came under my tutelage. I worked hard to prepare students for performing and learning what to do beyond the most thorough basic mastery of the music. This was always the ideal, this "mastery." The reality of a studio in a relatively affluent suburban area, where students have a great number of choices of activities, often provided less than an ideal environment, however, because there was little time left to give the necessary energy and commitment to practicing any instrument enough to succeed.

One could argue that teaching performance takes up all of the available time in traditional music lessons. It is the reason so many adults today say that, although they had years of lessons in their youth, they can't play anything in their maturity, not even the long-forgotten performance pieces. They seem to lack skills for independent study.

I believe that the balance needed to equip students for independent learning has to include a solid foundation in music theory, reading, and improvisation. Being able to make music oneself is unique. Learning to listen to music appreciatively, whether from a recording or from attendance at a live concert, makes for audiences who complete a sort of circle of communication among performers, who bring a score to life, and listeners who may be inspired and moved by it at any given time.

I also believe that the elephant in the living room (or the studio) is that to develop all of these aspects of a well-rounded musician is nearly impossible with half-hour weekly lessons and occasional, or even regular, group meetings. It is actually quite remarkable what so many teachers accomplish today in light of the limitations of time.

What does a teacher want students to do when their performances don't turn out the way they had planned? In my studio, we always emphasized that the show must go on, no matter what. One strategy was to "bail out," to finish the performance gracefully, if not accurately.

Teachers often teach best what was most difficult for them to learn. I discovered that many teachers often overlook an entire aspect of teaching performance—the sharing of piano playing. They are often surprised by a student's performance that "flopped." They might say, "I can't imagine why it didn't go well. You played perfectly yesterday. You really know that piece." As a friend of mine suggested, that's like holding the student out over an abyss all alone to deal with the problem. Everybody knows, these days, that the fear of performing is almost universal and that there is a multitude of solutions out there. Experts have given us preparatory exercises for focusing, for concentrating, even for embracing our fears (for anxiety and fear go together), in order to channel our energies in a positive way. And we have shared the manifestations of our excitement gone amuck, of the debilitating symptoms of our fears, and so on. It wasn't always so. The generational difference here is that now we can talk about it; we don't feel so "freaky" that we are anxious, vaguely guilty, and inadequate when we recognize performance anxiety in ourselves.

There is so much more information these days about this monster that stalks us and keeps us from doing our best. Think of it–our best would almost automatically appear with joy if we could only rise above the problem to peak performance, at least now and then!

Nearly everyone has a story. Scholar, philosopher, and human-capacity researcher Jean Houston says that we seek relationships with people's stories that parallel, advance, or complete our own:

Relationships spark and crackle in the telling and the hearing of shared stories....all relationships are ultimately a dance of constantly changing energies, frequencies, vibrations. Set a string vibrating and listen as an entire scale is heard—not just a single note but all its overtones.

Tell a good story, and discover that it contains all stories—not just in the actions recounted but, as in music, in the relationships between the notes, the silences, the rhythms. We are that string, and when we are plucked by the hand of story, we vibrate an entire scale.[1]

So it is that I offer my story. I hope that anyone who teaches music performance would benefit from reading what I have written. I hope it resonates enough with others' stories to offer insights that may alleviate unnecessary suffering and open up the experience of performing to the joy of sharing. I hope it will inspire someone else to dig to the roots and find some relief.

I

Seeds Sown in Uncertain Ground

Background

The Beginning

*I*t was at the Hamilton House. Gleaming in the sunshine, the slim white pillars bespoke an older day. The plantation-style, once-upon-a-time home could have been surrounded by huge oak trees forming the traditional grand entrance up the green to the steps of the wraparound porch.

Instead, refusing to fade away, the house had adapted itself to the city, which had grown up around it. Where green grass once grew, now asphalt streets and busy neighborhoods radiated the summer heat. White wicker furniture cluttered the porch, where guests in what was now the tearoom gathered in hopes of more air moving than the fans inside provided. This was a place for concerts, club meetings, and weddings.

The little girl with very dark brown hair stood behind her mother's chair on the shady porch. Her solo recital had just concluded. Her mother and the guests who had come to hear the little girl play the piano gathered on the porch to sip their ice-cold lemonade. The afternoon was warm—no, downright hot. The year was 1943, in the days before air conditioning. A wrap-around porch was the coolest place to be, if you could call it that, on a July afternoon in Texas. There was always the possibility of a breeze.

The little pianist was nine years old. She had studied piano for only a year. Her mother had sewn her simple, pale yellow, cotton eyelet dress, just right for a steamy summer day. It set off her deep tan. Much to her delight, the special recital dress extended all the way to the floor, and she loved it!

Her teacher had even provided a lovely printed program listing all of the pieces she would play. It was made from an 11" x 6¾" piece of paper folded so that it would open like a little book to 3½" x 5½" as if to say, tastefully, "This is a little program presented by a little girl. Please enjoy." The front looked like this:

PIANO RECITAL

By

NANCY BLAKEN

**Pupil of
Mrs. Robert C. Jones**

**Wednesday Evening
July 14, 1943**

Hamilton House

On the inside right was the program, and on the left side was a charming poem by Hilda Conkling. It was elegant, and it made the young performer feel incredibly special:

MUSIC

If I think music,

It comes and goes

If the fountain ripples and splashes

It keeps on singing.

Falling broken water

Sings and answers

When the warblers in the May trees

Stay close for a little

But the music that I hear

Is different in its meaning...

Happy hour or sorrowing

Into change

PROGRAM

Evening Prayer. . . . . .F. Arthur Johnson

Sonatina in G . . . . Beethoven

Minuet . . . . Bach

(from Anna Magdalena's Notebook)

Tippy-Toe . . . . Humphreys

The Lonely Organ Grinder . . . . .Diller

My Red Umbrella. . . . . .Frost

Triads at Play . . . . Fox

Valse . . . . Sprenger

Little Piano Pieces by a Little Girl . . . . .Barbara Jones

> **The Birdies Are Singing**
> **Little Bird Hopping**
> **Lullaby, Baby**
> **I Saw a Ship A-Sailing**

Folk-Tunes and Melodies from the opera "Hansel and Gretel"
by Humperdinck. Arranged for piano by Jeanne Boylen.

> **Susy, Little Susy**
> **Come Dance With Me**
> **The Elf-Man**
> **When At Night I Go to Sleep**
> **Happiness**

My, what an occasion! It had been so much fun to play all her favorite pieces for an audience. She felt bathed in joy that day—imagine, sharing your very own music making!

The Metaphoric Self

Everyone knows the charm of early childhood innocence. Unselfconscious, spontaneous, curious, the emotionally healthy child has the world by the tail. She simply can't wait to experience what tomorrow has in store for her. Learning with her whole body, her joy will most likely take form in jumping, wiggling, and expressing herself in space rather than only in mind and voice. Opposite emotions, of course, are displayed just as easily.

Metaphor and free association, making connections between the seen and the unseen, are always present, though not necessarily understood. I once knew an articulate three-year-old who had been involved in performances from both sides—stage and audience—who exclaimed, upon seeing a seedy slice of watermelon, "Look, an audience of seeds!"

A YouTube video (2010) of remarkable three-year-old Jonathan conducting a recording of Beethoven's fifth symphony astonished the world. The gestures inherent in the music were all there—the intimacy of quiet, less dense parts (tiny hand gestures, pulling in of the body), the exuberance of the *tutti* (jumping up and down, waving arms wildly), the broad, sweeping lyricism (waving arms in big arcs). When conductor Jonathan lost his baton at the end, he squealed with delight and collapsed off his little platform in a paroxysm of laughter, totally appropriate for his age, free and unrestrained in his joy. This is what children love to do before they are schooled to sit still and to express themselves only intellectually.

Humans have a natural capacity to think in images (metaphors). Common to many cultures, this capacity is perhaps universal in young children but usually is reduced greatly by an emphasis on verbal processes in Western culture. Many children are natural visualizers but often become cut off from their visualizing by the verbal–linear processes imposed by the

6

educational system. The process of using visual imagery is especially creative because it tends to gather meanings, seek solutions, and organize learning into symbolic drama or narrative. The repeated use of vivid, narrative imagery is inclined to increase the motivation to be creative. It gets to be a habit!

The desire to share is a natural attempt to connect with another person. A child spontaneously wants to tell someone, "Look! Look what I can do!" "Look, Mom, no hands!" The drawing brought home from kindergarten is presented lovingly. The piano piece, polished at the lesson, is played again for anyone who will listen, or a new piece has been assigned. "Look at my new piece!"

Stewart Gordon, writing in *Etudes for Piano Teachers,* talks about the frequent preoccupation among young students with reaching virtuosity (loud and fast!) and its appropriateness to childhood.

> *Like physical growing itself, there seems to be a period in one's development which is devoted primarily to getting this job done.*
>
> *As teachers and musicians, we might even heartily applaud this unbridled preoccupation with virtuosity—up to a point. This is not to say that with maturation, other qualities should not take the dominant role and supplant the virtuosity craze...but in that youthful burst of energy we might as well join the crowd, enjoy the show, and encourage our youngsters to revel in the laurels of this kind of heroism.[1]*

If you are a music teacher, maybe each of your students needs to learn a piece that could be played wholeheartedly and with abandon, "raising the roof" for the sheer joy of virtuosity now and then. But you need to be authentic in your own enthusiasm for a piece of music. If you can love it yourself, even at an elementary level (like "Great Smoky Mountains" by

David Carr Glover, with triads all over the piano keyboard, both *forte* and *piano* sections) and if you have two pianos, just think how much fun it is for your student to come in the door and have you say about a piece the student knows very well, "Let's play 'Smoky' together for a warm-up!" Both of you will totally love the big sound, feel important, and maybe even giggle companionably.

Many other student pieces are exciting, dramatic, and rhythmic. The enjoyment is universal. Tarantellas are good examples. Add the legend of the tarantella dance of Gypsies to dispel the spider's poison, and the student is "hooked." Exciting and enthusiastic playing in the earliest years can pave the way for a maturing performer to communicate the marvel of music profoundly.

I found it difficult to plan a season's repertoire when the right moment to present a piece like this could hardly be predetermined. That is why I wanted to have a special piece on hand in the studio to issue as a slightly easier reward for a project well done, rather than sending the student's parent to the music store to buy it.

The seeds sown in my early years bound me forever to a love for musical expression at the piano. My personal musical journey, like that of many others, is a story of the acquisition of skills as well as of the blocks to gaining those skills at optimal points in my development. Performance skills, which give us the means for sharing emotions and wonders of great music, begin with the first lessons and spiral upward from days, weeks, years of introduction to and immersion in styles of expression beyond words.

What happens to the vitality and enthusiasm of childhood? What happened to the little girl in the yellow dress? William Westney, in *The Perfect Wrong Note*, addresses this question:

Sometimes musical vitality blossoms into vivid expressivity as a person grows up. Sometimes it is taken for granted, or its exuberance is dismissed as babyish. Sometimes it gradually withers away from neglect. Sometimes it is flattened by the insensitive remarks of a teacher, parent, or peer. In any event, vitality seems surprisingly perishable, despite its naturalness, and it requires nurturing in order to thrive.[2]

Getting Ready

The recital was on the forty-first birthday of the little girl's mother. Her father was away, teaching at a college summer camp. Neither her brother nor her sister was present at the event. It wasn't a family affair. Perhaps that was simply typical of a time when parents were not as involved in their children's activities as they are now in the first decades of the twenty-first century. Her mother's letter of July 7th to her father about a group (studio) recital suggests the importance, or lack thereof, of their children's activities.

This coming Saturday evening Mrs. Jones is having another musical event: The group that did the little Hansel and Gretel act at the recital is going to repeat the performance at the Jones home. I don't imagine it will last very long but am bothered about its being on Sat. night.

I don't know when you're coming and don't want to use up a Sat. evening that way. It may be that one or both of us can deliver her there and she could call us when it's over.

It turned out that this performance was canceled, as indicated in a PS to the same letter:

No recital for Sat. evening. Latest bulletin.

9

Previously, in the same letter, the little girl's father had been given the date for the solo recital:

> Nancy's recital is to be Wednesday evening, July 14th, the only date that could be arranged before Mrs. Jones's vacation. It is to be a brief and simple affair for the purpose of giving Nancy the experience, not for any display of her unusual (?) talents.

Years later, when the mature student discovered these letters, she wondered whether Mrs. Jones had at some time previously experienced the disappointment of parents who thought their child was a budding virtuoso because he or she had given a solo recital. Perhaps she was being especially cautious about building up expectations. She very likely contributed to the parents' lingering inability to support the importance of piano in the life of the little girl in the yellow dress.

What was it like for her mother to host this daughter's recital on her own birthday? Probably, it was something close to an ordinary social occasion. At home there was no birthday tradition of parties with so many people around. Birthdays were usually celebrated by opening presents at breakfast time. In any case, at that time, little attention was given to the specialness of birthdays or recitals, at least compared to the more child-centered, family celebrations of seventy years later!

In a letter written one day prior to the recital, the girl's mother included one sentence about the upcoming occasion to her father: "Tomorrow is Nancy's recital, so the time will be devoted to preparation." In subsequent daily letters, the discussion was about details of an imminent move, house hunting in a new town, and problems associated with packing. No mention was made of the occasion of the recital. Presumably it went well. It simply was not important enough to comment on in light of other matters.

Fifty-four years passed. Memories faded. The now-mature musician could hardly remember ever having accomplished such a feat as playing a solo recital so early in her musical studies.

Visiting her mother just before her mother's move to a retirement facility, she went to the garage on a warm and damp afternoon with instructions to look through a box of the remnants of her childhood and select what she wanted to keep, if anything. The cool garage smelled musty. Boxes were piled around the walls in an orderly fashion, stacked on board shelves supported by bricks. It was important to keep them above the damp concrete floor, where mold would have destroyed the cardboard. They contained a little of everything—old utility-bill stubs, bits of carefully rolled string, books, magazines, records of the whereabouts of rocks collected, and field trips taken (her father was a geologist), letters, and programs of events.

There it was, in the middle of the dusty concrete floor—a box of miscellaneous papers reflecting her childhood. When she picked up the small, mold-stained, folded recital program, recognition hit her suddenly.

"I knew I had played a piano recital all by myself when I was very young!" Suddenly, she saw years stretched out as if in a long line, dreamlike, with a length of white twine laid across them connecting the day of the solo recital to the present time. She had indeed been a serious, eager little student after all and had accomplished enough to present a solo recital very early in her studies. Her blurry memory of the event was real. She had her answer. When she had asked about it periodically, her mother hadn't been able to remember.

Children of the Times

For anyone who was born and raised during The Great Depression and its aftermath in the United States, the remnants of a Victorian attitude toward children abounded. Children were treated as objects. "Don't praise them too much or they will grow up conceited." (an epithet seldom used today). Household rules were strict, and schedules were ironclad. The opinions of children were considered unimportant, if voiced at all, and certainly not to be taken seriously. Parents were absolute authorities on any subject, especially on proper behavior.

Lurking beneath that atmosphere was the assumption that men were always right and that women were to remember their places. Children were expected to excel in school, especially if they were the offspring of well-educated parents; they were not to be conspicuous but rather, to keep quiet about their accomplishments.

After a political discussion with her father on a visit home during her sophomore year in college, the budding young lady was improperly argumentative. She was told, "You'll never get a husband that way!"

This suggests a fascinating description by psychoanalyst Alice Miller (*The Drama of the Gifted Child*) of thwarted emotional fulfillment, or development, in adults who "cathect" their condition on their children. Because it was the norm to deny expression of emotions on the basis that they were signs of weakness, the idea that parents often projected their own emotional needs on children comes as no surprise. Miller says that this in no way precludes parents' ability to love their children; it only indicates that they sometimes desperately need them to behave in a certain way.

There was little understanding in the early part of the 1900s of the developmental stages of childhood, much less of the need to develop healthy self-esteem and confidence in one's personal worth—behavioral characteristics of these stages. What we don't resolve in our own emotional development, writes Miller, we can easily look to our children to provide for us. A child is at her mother's (or father's) "disposal...and can be so brought up that it becomes what she wants it to be. A child can be made to show respect." The parents can impose their own feelings on her and "see themselves mirrored" in her love and admiration.[3]

Darkness and Light

She put the book down suddenly. "Not good bedtime reading," she said out loud. The book was the biography, Isak Dineson, *by Judith Thurman, and she had just read that the "central drama of her [Dineson's] life" was the attempt to resolve the contradictions between her parents and how they were raised, what their families represented. No wonder her mother's treasured hardback copy, now in her hands, included clippings of newspaper articles about Dineson, and no wonder her mother had collected several volumes of this famous author's work.*

She wasn't going to relax and sleep easily with the bombardment of thoughts this discovery of the so called "central drama" evoked. The expectation to excel while being quiet about it if one were female turned out to present an important conflict in her own life as she struggled with presenting herself in performance while being admonished to be inconspicuous.

She remembered that her parents were in constant conflict when she was growing up. The young musician remembered that in her teen years, when she had been invited to spend a night with a friend, she had noticed how nice the parents were to each other and how relaxed they seemed. She had discovered that not everyone needed to live the way her own parents did.

In their later years, a kind of truce evolved between her mother and father. Their mutual enjoyment of travel and sophisticated humor kept their lives interesting. Gone were the problems of raising children and of balancing privacy with twenty years of a resident elderly aunt's constant interference with their business.

Her parents were certainly the products of the waning Victorian Age. Add to that their access to higher education at first-rate institutions and, for her father, a doctorate in science. Their lack of what today would be called "emotional education" and their attitude that "children are to be seen and not heard," as well as, "little pitchers have big ears," was not at all unusual. Nor was her father's admonition, "Just remember, women were put here to help men."

It was years before she fully came to appreciate her parents' positive legacy— that of absolute connection to nature and its creatures manifested in their love for the outdoors. From her father she learned democracy of human interaction, the importance of striving for moral integrity, commitment to hard work, and the obligation to try to leave the world a better place. Her father believed that he carried a mantle of superior knowledge and educational privilege and was thus obligated to fulfill that ideal.

Her mother's legacy included curiosity, a deep sense of humor (including nonsense), joie de vivre, a great love of music, books, and reading, and most of all, the drive to survive.

The parents of the little girl in the yellow dress came from a time in which the breakup of a family by divorce was unthinkable. Better to raise children in the meanness of constant conflict, no matter what the circumstances, than to separate family members. The gold standard of virtue was reached by "sticking to it."

Tall, dark, and handsome, the little girl's father was intriguing and brilliant, shy and mysterious, when he met her mother. He came from a strict family of German origin. He was captivated by a woman who could talk intelligently on any number of subjects, shared his love of nature, and was anything but meekly acquiescent. He was not wise enough, however, to see the inherent conflict that this would bring to a relationship in which his authority would be challenged constantly. No doubt, like many of his contemporaries, he was torn between wanting the "helpmeet" wife and enjoying the companionship of a well-educated and independent partner.

To this relationship he brought a dark and tormenting burden—deep shame and guilt. He was the only "good" son out of three who grew to adulthood. His mother, kind and enduring but steeped in religious piety and inflexibility, was dying of a broken heart. She had raised three children out of six to adulthood; her beautiful daughter died at age seven from the aftereffects of measles. Today we would likely diagnose the oldest son as depressed and give him treatment. He deserted his family and was never heard from again. The youngest son, spoiled and charming, rebelled and left for the west. Both of these sons, like the young pianist's father, had married stable, smart, "survivor" women.

His mother had made it clear to her "good" son that he was the only one who turned out right, and he was all she had after her husband died. In one of her letters, she reminded him: "As I have frequently told you, you are our only solace."

The family business, once a thriving classic fin de siècle *confectionery and ice cream shop, had gone bankrupt. The accompanying shame and guilt the family felt then is unimaginable today, when people often declare bankruptcy*

15

to avoid having to pay overcharged credit card bills. But there it was. It's all in the letters. The little girl's grandmother wrote to her son in 1918:

> Papa is sore beset—what to do to earn a living.
>
> The Provident Co. foreclosed on the buildings—that means that they bought them for the price of the mortgage they held, accrued interest and taxes…. It means that nearly all of [our] money has been lost in the business.

Years later, the little-girl—now grown up—would decide that this family shame would bear investigating. Perhaps there was a connection between these emotions and her musical experience.

There was another side to the father of the little girl in the yellow dress that influenced her growing up in a very positive way. The fun times were Sunday afternoon family outings—unless something came up to cause conflict. Generally, though, her daddy was mellow and gentle on these occasions because he loved being outdoors most of all. Usually the children and their father explored some creek or river or remote parkland. And sometimes, because "trespassing" was not in the vocabulary of farmers and ranchers much in those days, they traversed pastures to find what they were looking for.

They traipsed over a hill once to dig in the loamy soil for special fossils called ammonites—a species of ancient spiral-chambered nautilus. They were detectives, treasure hunters. The newly turned earth was pungent and dark. Little grubs didn't like having their pleasant afternoon disturbed, but they were paid no mind. Trees were showing their spring chartreuse, shimmering in the breeze. Cows in the pasture chewed their cuds lazily and stared at the intruders, wondering "What were those weird people digging for beside my water hole?"

"Here we are!" the father exclaimed. The fossils were exposed. Some were giant, some were medium in size. Only the little ones were complete.

The family speculated that the large pieces must have come from a circular whole about the size of a bicycle tire. The children could see suture marks in the limestone. They happily lugged as many fossils as they could carry back to the car and took them home. This was the source of the positive legacy, of the little girl's sense of curiosity and of wonder, her at-homeness in nature, as well as her love of teaching. "How did you know there would be ammonites over that ridge, Daddy?"

"Oh, I just had a hunch." That's when he was happiest, at least in her memory. That's when she did not have to worry about his mercurial, stern moods and felt comfortable in his presence.

The Piano and the Little Girl

She had waited interminably to begin piano lessons. Once, when she had been invited to go home after school with her friend, Suzanne, she discovered a beautiful, small, and shiny spinet piano in the living room. Heading for the bench right away, she squashed down flat handfuls of keys. On the piano at home, she had already found the pedal. Now her foot went down automatically. What fun! She imagined she had on a flowing gown and was a famous pianist performing on a stage. The sounds smeared and roared from beneath her hands, and she was lost in delight. This piano was much prettier than the one at home, although the sound wasn't nearly so full.

The big "elephant" piano at home was in the hallway downstairs. It stood tall and had a lined, sun-damaged skin, tough black/brown, with real ivory keys that were yellowing. Her mother often played after her daughter had gone to bed. Sounds of Rachmaninoff, Beethoven, Chaminade, Sibelius, and Rubenstein filled the evenings. She loved listening to her mother. Later she would find, in a treasured home journal written by her grandfather in 1917, that her mother's early Philadelphia childhood had included many opportunities to hear orchestras, recitals, operas, and plays.

One of the best things about Christmas was caroling around the piano with her mother playing. It was just before bedtime and just after cookies and milk had been put out for Santa. She remembered marveling as she stood beside her mother, wishing she could play, too. Then, at some point, her mother's playing ceased. Perhaps it was after a move to another town. They never talked about it.

Finally, the day came for the little girl's first piano lesson. Her mother went with her the first time; after that she rode the city bus all by herself. She eagerly approached Mrs. Jones's home. She had expected to go to a big piano at this teacher's house as soon as she arrived, but at first they sat at a card table and made tents with their hands gently rounded on the table. Then the teacher gave her a music book, a red book that was wider than it was tall. It was filled with little ink sketches of children, animals, parades, special flowers, and music to go with them. The little girl could hardly wait to get started!

Home again, she looked all through the book and imagined how she would make music with all of the pieces she would soon learn to play. It was always that way—she examined any new book eagerly, as if she could already hear how the music would describe the pictures. Every now and then, she would play all of the pieces she had ever studied and could hardly believe she had learned so many.

A Different Day

As a teacher, I was often surprised at the apparent lack of musical curiosity of many of my students. After the introduction of a new music book, it seemed to me that the first week at home might have involved exploring its contents. We could have done this together during the lesson, though we did not always have time after I made and explained an assignment. At the next meeting, I would say, "Did you peek?" and they would shake their heads to say no. Were students forbidden to look ahead in their school material? Today's students seem more likely, swamped with homework as they are, to do only what they are told and to be concerned with getting everything right and no more. I remembered that earlier in my teaching career, students were a little more relaxed and curious to see what was next.

On a more positive note, today's music teachers often provide many opportunities for students of all ages to perform both formally and informally. My own studio, with a number of adult students, held a potluck supper occasionally at someone's home, and everyone played or just listened. Camaraderie bubbled up easily when the students commiserated about the problems of performing. When a performer looked at her own music and said, "I've never seen this before!" supportive laughter broke out.

Younger students can play in a "living composer" festival. This idea has been around for years but is perhaps more widely known now. It can be a rewarding and motivating event for a student. Playing the music for the composer who wrote it is thrilling. The composer's autograph on the music makes him or her a minor celebrity in the student's (and the teacher's) eyes.

⎯⎯⎯◞

Mrs. Jones was a very active teacher and provided many opportunities for her students to perform. One afternoon the little girl, a beginning pianist now, left school early to play for the composer Stanley Sprenger. She was absolutely awestruck that Mr. Sprenger had written a piece she could play, that children all over the country could play. She had thought all composers living at the same time she did would write only music that was out of her reach. Meeting a live composer was special, not to mention playing for someone who knew music was a big part of life. She wore a "Sunday dress" to school that day so she would be ready to play for Mr. Sprenger afterward. How one dressed for a special event mattered a lot. Special clothing seemed to say "This is important!"

19

The event was held at an old house full of beautiful furniture and velvet drapes. She went into a cozy, softly lit room where there was a lovely brown grand piano just waiting for her. And there sat Mr. Sprenger with a smile to greet her. She just knew he really wanted to hear her play his piece. (She would realize one day that playing pieces by composer Mr. William Gillock, while he listened and wrote comments, must have been equally impressive to her students.)

There were other studio recitals (although independent music teachers' home teaching spaces weren't called "studios" then) and, of course, the annual auditions of the early years of the National Guild of Piano Teachers. The first time the little girl traveled twenty-five miles with her teacher to the big city where Guild was headquartered, she played in a teacher's home. One of the pieces was "The Swan." It was a beautiful and graceful piece, and she could imagine that the sounds she played were just like a swan gliding through the water. Years afterward, she could still see the piano keys and feel the comfort of playing a piece she knew so well. What an adventure!

Then Mrs. Jones suggested to her mother that the little girl give a solo recital. The little girl who would soon have a lovely yellow dress hadn't realized that she knew enough pieces to play a recital all by herself. What a wonderful idea! She eagerly joined her teacher in planning which pieces she would play and what order would make a nice program. Little did she know that her teacher and her mother would soon get busy talking about how to find a pleasant place with a good, grand piano and how to determine a guest list. Who among her mother's friends would be interested in supporting such an endeavor? Who would simply enjoy hearing an accomplished little girl share her music?

Interruption

After the beginning year of lessons, though, and not long after that special solo recital, the family moved to a new town where there would be a new teacher. This time it was the dean of the Music Department at the local university. "This should sound like the whipped cream on strawberry short-cake," he would say in his gentle voice. She was enchanted when he said things like that. She knew exactly what he meant. There were lots of new pieces to play, too, and it seemed that they quickly became much harder and more impressive.

Learning the Beethoven Rondo in C Major, op. 51, no. 1, was especially difficult, partly because, while she liked it well enough, she didn't love it, and she dragged her feet practicing it. (When she became a teacher herself, she realized that at the time she hadn't understood this music at all. It was likely beyond the scope of her musical experience.) She finally completed it and played it on several occasions.

One evening at supper time, the doorbell rang. It was Dr. Mercer. This kind gentleman, one of her parents' friends in addition to being her piano teacher, had come to the house bearing a little chocolate cake with white icing. On it, written in red icing, was "Rondo in C." By that time, though, the girl was not proud of the piece. She felt she hadn't really played it well. She had taken so long to learn it, and she didn't really love it the way she had loved other pieces. Somehow, she felt she had let Dr. Mercer down. He seemed to think this Beethoven piece was a gem. Maybe he was disappointed that she didn't really share his enthusiasm. She felt she didn't deserve the special attention. Although she didn't understand it yet, she felt like an imposter. This vague feeling was the beginning of guilt and shame associated with performing music and took the edge off the joy of the occasion.

Changes

Piano pedagogy has undergone major changes in the past fifty years, of course. In the forties and later, in the training of the little girl in the yellow dress, teaching by demonstration alone was still the order of the day. "Here, play it like this!" the teacher would say. Theory was taught separately, often completely away from the instrument, and mentioned only casually at lessons. Most importantly, students who learned to read music quickly, and the little girl in the yellow dress was one of them, were given whatever level of music they could read and play with an appropriate degree of skill. The meaning, gesture, and emotional content of the music were not talked about often. It was assumed that when a student played expressively, or musically, he or she was a "natural," born to it. Students who were these "naturals" were praised for being "musical" and were considered especially talented.

We know now that even though many students do indeed have a special affinity for the language of music and an intuitive ability to play expressively, musicality can be cultivated from the beginning lessons. True, students are more likely to be musical if they have *heard* good music from their earliest years, either from their home environments or from exposure to special programs designed for early childhood. Teaching how to practice and how to use one's imagination are also important elements.

Practicing

How about the art of practicing? Few teachers paid attention to teaching *how* to practice effectively until recent decades. How do we go about this? Lessons can be models of how to work at home to help students avoid simply playing their pieces over and over again. Beginning students, even prereading ones, can identify and listen to parts or sections that sound almost alike but with small changes, to patterns that repeat, or to dynamic contrasts. Lots of different ways to practice small parts can be explored at lessons so that students can hear their playing improve. They can share in making decisions about how the music might sound, laying the groundwork for more sophisticated analysis.

If I were teaching the little girl today, I might ask her to show me how she had practiced a particular passage so I could check in on what was going on between lessons. I might ask her to record a home practice session. I might ask her why she thinks a certain passage or figure seems to be more difficult than others, why she always makes a mistake in a certain place and what she could do about that, why it's more difficult to memorize this or that passage than some others, or what would happen if she practiced certain spots in the music very slowly. I could ask, "what do you fingers *want* to do?," to discover reasons for mistakes. I would talk about solutions with her instead of just showing her how to do it. I would ask *her* to demonstrate for *me*, encouraging an assumption that problems can be solved.

Unfortunately, many lessons are performances of a sort, so that the teacher can hear what is good and accurate and what needs to be worked on, to be played again this way or that way (as in the traditional master class).

When a student is preparing for a performance, though, practicing *performing* is certainly the business of a lesson. All the elements of careful and thoughtful practice leading up to that performance are now ready to come together in an exciting presentation.

Understanding how music works—theory—is important to practicing productively. Teaching theory completely apart from playing the instrument, as was the case in the education of the little girl, makes it harder to relate concepts to pieces. Nowadays, all major curriculum systems include theory from the ground up. At every level, these books of concepts with examples prepare students to analyze the elements of music, give them tools to compose their own pieces, and often begin with stories illustrated by the music.

Thinking about how music can communicate does not need to be limited to advancing students. For example, so much music written for the purpose of teaching young students imitates and describes animal sounds or moods such as anger, sadness, joy, etc. What are the technical details that might help tell the stories? (Here's where big, dynamic contrasts come in.) What do sudden changes tell us? What does a slur express? How important is an ending? Many current instruction books and special publications offer sound and specific practice suggestions in great detail.[4]

Making the connection between a piece's title and its descriptive message is one of the elements of understanding music. I once heard William Gillock, a beloved composer of music for teaching that delights young students and prepares them for masterwork styles, tell a story about a young beginner who played his composition, "Flamenco," at an event he was adjudicating. After her performance of dreamy, slow, heavily pedaled music, he asked her what she thought the title of the piece referred to. Her answer: "Oh, it's one of those long-legged pink birds."

There is a neurological component, as Daniel Coyle writes in his 2009 book, *The Talent Code,* that supports an analytical approach to practice. He describes, in layman's terms, how a substance called "myelin" wraps itself around certain nerve fibers, or circuits, when they are put to use. Myelin is the physiological basis of skill development. "Deep practice," mindfully gleaning information about what causes mistakes, makes changing and correcting them optimal. The acquisition of any skill, whether it is artistic or athletic, involves working through mistakes intentionally.

> *Struggle is not optional—it's neurologically required: In order to get your skill circuit to fire optimally, [correct mistakes] you must by definition fire the circuit suboptimally; you must make mistakes and pay attention to those mistakes; you must slowly teach your circuit. You must also keep firing that circuit—i.e., practicing.... To sum up: It's time to rewrite the maxim that practice makes perfect. The truth is, practice makes myelin, and myelin makes perfect.*[5]

This approach to practice, of course, is what noted author William Westney refers to as "the perfect wrong note," the one that gives information about what one needs to practice. Honest mistakes, *pure* mistakes, happen. What we do about them makes all the difference. *Careless* mistakes are ones we ignore and don't pay attention to right away. Here is what Westney says about honest mistakes:

> *Honest mistakes form the quickest way, the healthiest way, to learning that is authentic and solid. Best of all, the process of working through honest mistakes has vital, positive energy because it grows out of an attitude of healthy self-acceptance…. [Honest mistakes] often have a sophisticated knack for revealing the underlying, specific reason for a particular glitch—a reason the conscious mind may not have considered.*[6]

Add to this Malcom Gladwell's concept, in *Outliers,* of the 10,000 hours it takes to become an expert,[7] and one can see the results of much current thinking and research into age-old issues about practicing. Westney looks at practicing then and now, devoting a whole chapter called "Juicy Mistakes" in *The Perfect Wrong Note* to effective practicing.

Even though various authors have written about insights like these recently, I believe that the best teachers and the most serious students have always known these approaches to practice, some intuitively and some intellectually. My own understanding, as the little girl with quite respectable and credentialed teachers in the early years of her musical training, was that practice was simply repetition of passages and sections, often beginning again when mistakes were made (when a student says, "C'n I start over?") or at least hurriedly correcting them (a kind of musical stuttering). No one ever checked to see whether I understood or put to work any other kind of practice (not even at the college level). *Mistakes were sources of embarrassment and shame, to be avoided at all costs.*

Imagination

Imagination nurtures the interpretation of music. It can open up secrets of expression that await within both student and instrument. ("How

25

many different sounds can I play?") Certainly some individuals are more imaginative than others, but after all, one of the supreme elements of all art is imagination. In the explosion of fine instructional materials of the past decade or two, a great deal of attention has been given to teaching not only how to analyze and practice efficiently but also how to explore interpretive elements. This exploration is accompanied by lovely, artistic illustrations that are tasteful and do not distract from the musical score by dominating the page.

I was working once with a precocious eleven-year-old student on Mozart's Fantasy in D Minor, K. 397, and asked her to bring a story for the opening section to her next lesson. Anticipating angst and drama, I was eager to hear her ideas. It was not to be in those terms, however.

"This is where the monsters come up out of the deep," she said as she played the opening passage with a feeling of dark mystery played with rather sophisticated musical shaping. I celebrated her imagination both outwardly and inwardly and bit my tongue to keep from imposing on her my own ideas, lest I influence her too much.

What Is She Learning?

How do we informally determine what a student knows? How do we test him or her without saying, "Now we're going to have a test!" One way is to assign a piece to be learned completely independently (no help from parents or friends). Another is to ask a student to select his or her own piece among the materials at home (perhaps from books not completely used) and learn one as an "on your own" piece. Yet another is simply to ask questions of the student, lots of them, to find out what he or she is thinking. When the student is reluctant for fear of saying the wrong thing, we can offer several alternative answers quickly and ask which answer would be best.

Occasionally, too, students are so afraid of playing a wrong note that they avoid really sinking into the keys to make a rich sound. (This does not take into account the sometimes inferior instruments or even electronic keyboards used at home.) Often they have so little confidence in their own interpretations that they think playing loudly or softly is risky. Asking them to exaggerate dynamic markings—to "overdo it"—works well. This encourages experimenting in practice that sometimes turns out just right after they have been holding back. Thinking about it this way can help uncover students' own feelings about the music. The little girl in the yellow dress was often afraid of committing herself to a strong musical statement. What a waste! She and her teacher might have had an interesting discussion exploring the difference between nuance and more obvious expression.

Caution! If a conscientious parent, one who makes it a habit to pay attention to home practice, doesn't understand the assignment of exaggeration, he or she might criticize the student's effort and say, "Can't you play a little softer?" Or "Stop it! You're butchering that music!"

II

Buds and Weeds

Skills and Blockages

Moving On

*P*iano lessons with Dr. Mercer, more commonly known as "Dean"
Mercer because he was the dean of the local university's Department
of Music, were held in the nearby Methodist Church. It was not so far for
a twelve year-old to have to walk in the afternoon after school. And the
growing girl enjoyed exploring the maze-like corridors of the church after
her lesson was over. Children were quite accustomed to walking or riding
their bikes everywhere, anyway, from home to school or church or down-
town after school for a soda at the corner drugstore. Nothing seemed far
away from the town square, with its classic Victorian courthouse so typical of small-town Texas.

Even though she was almost a teenager, it was scary when she had to buy
new music. She went to buy the Schirmer editions, with their yellowish,
creamy covers lined with a narrow green design, from The Tavern, a book-
store on the small university campus. It always took lots of courage to go in
there where all the grown-up students were. Not so little anymore, she was
growing and changing. As she grew toward adolescence, she was increas-
ingly self-conscious and generally embarrassed about almost everything.

Shadows began to hover over her musical experience. First of all, because her
schooling had begun midwinter just after her sixth birthday, she was always
halfway through a school grade by the time September came around. In the
new, smaller town, the system didn't allow for that. Just as puberty loomed
in the foreground, she was skipped forward to the sixth grade. Everyone

was more mature, it seemed, and her already wobbly self-confidence hit the skids. As she moved into her teens, nothing, neither academic work nor music practice, seemed fun. She lost that childhood assurance that she could do well at anything and everything.

Playing a concerto with a fellow student was thrilling but daunting. She consistently felt unprepared and embarrassed. She was sure her fellow student partner, who always did everything right, was much better than she was. The teacher had assigned the orchestral reduction accompaniment to her and the solo part to her friend. They never completed or performed it. This first movement of Concerto in D Minor, op.40, by Mendelssohn, was beautiful, but even though she could play it, our musical girl didn't understand anything about concerti!

Here is a vignette that was typical of her experiences in that terribly self-conscious time.

Herr Schmitt lived across the side street from the not-so-little-anymore girl who played the piano. The windows were always open in both houses, so he could hear her practicing at the tall upright in her dining room. The street was narrow; it was a gravel road that ran between the sides of the houses. The Schmitts' house was set back considerably with a big front yard, and hers stood right at the corner.

Dr. and Mrs. Schmitt were refugees. They had weathered the Second World War in Germany, but they had sent their two sons away early to London. When the boys, now grown, came to join their parents for a grand reunion, it was to a new home in the United States, where Dr. Schmitt had found a job as a professor of chemistry at the local university. Dr. Schmitt played the violin. He and his wife, Elsa, were good friends and neighbors to the young pianist's parents. He suggested that it would be nice to play piano and violin together. Apparently, when he had heard the piano playing through the open windows, he thought a classical duet was quite in order. He came over one

31

day with his music. The girl was mortified. She thought she couldn't sight read music adequately. She stumbled around at the keyboard, missing notes and not wanting to admit that she didn't really know how to count this Mozart. She was too afraid to ask for help and too embarrassed to admit that she needed it. She was "all thumbs." Besides, Herr Schmitt seemed a little strange, with his thick German accent.

Years later, she would remember this, thinking how much fun it might have been to make music with Herr Schmitt. Maybe she could have offered to practice the music by herself and call him when she was ready. Or maybe she could have asked her teacher to help her with it. Why had she not been able to reach out and ask for help?

Herr Schmitt did not visit again. Perhaps he asked of himself, "Why inflict upon this child a task that seemed to embarrass her so?"

Accompanying and Ensemble Skills

What an opportunity for the little girl in the yellow dress, sadly missed! If I were teaching her today, I could encourage her to play with Herr Schmitt and to take a look at the music to see if the level were appropriate, not so difficult that it would take all of her practice time. Of course this would require a level of communication already established between us so that she could share with me the invitation to play with Herr Schmitt. If the music were too demanding, I could help her find a more accessible number, and perhaps together we could see if Herr Schmitt would be agreeable. Maybe they could perform an ensemble at the next studio recital, enhancing the sense of musical community for everyone.

Students are often asked to accompany a choir at school, and they bring the music to a lesson for help. Together, the teacher and student need to assess the difficulty, how a piece can be worked into repertoire plans for the year, etc. The responsibility for agreeing to such a request or saying, "No thank you, not this year" belongs to student and teacher, not the school faculty who spot an accomplished student and want, or need, to take advantage of those abilities.

Students who learn to accompany are in demand. They can derive lots of pleasure and a sense of accomplishment from reading and learning the music. Their performance poise and self-assurance likely will be enhanced. There's a distinction, though, between this skill and that of playing a part in an original chamber music piece. Again, it's crucial that the teacher and the student have established healthy communication by the time these situations come up.

No Direction

The young adolescent became a lazy practicer. Sometimes on a sunny afternoon after school, when she was supposed to practice, she would lie down on the bench and play a Hanon exercise with one hand so her mother would think she was still working. She didn't know how to practice anyway—most students didn't in those days. They simply read the notes and repeated them.

With other students, she attended a theory class weekly. It was held in a tiny Sunday School classroom without a piano. Theory seemed abstract. It was boring, and she drifted away. She knew later, from marks penciled on her music long before, that she had been exposed to theory at her private lessons. But it certainly didn't take. No one ever checked to see whether she understood, whether she "got it."

Perhaps a blockage about really learning to play began then. Several times, when she practiced a Mozart sonata, she noticed that the end sounded like the beginning, but she could not have described the parts of sonata form or the change of keys in the Recapitulation. She never liked any of the endings, as a matter of fact, because she didn't understand the key changes or even the concept of key. The beginnings always sounded more familiar, so naturally, the repetition of the themes introduced in the first part and recurring later in different keys never sounded right.

Somehow the music she was learning was no longer exciting. She still felt passionate about music and loved to go to recitals and concerts, but she didn't really enjoy the pieces she was asked to learn. Dean Mercer tactfully told her parents he no longer had room for her and negotiated with them to transfer her lessons to his colleague, a very nice and beautiful, but not passionate, lady. Her parents were not fooled. They pointed out to her that because she didn't work at piano, the dean was no longer interested. She was vaguely ashamed. Conscious only that her face felt hot, she wanted to look away from the conversation until she could leave the room and be alone, a familiar situation when her inadequacies were brought to her attention.

Things picked up for a while with the new teacher, though. Performance activities continued, including annual Guild auditions. Recitals were always held at the local university library auditorium on a big stage with a beautiful black grand piano. After the programs, all of the students posed for a group picture on the stage. These were special occasions to which the girls wore formal gowns all the way to the floor. Once the young girl's grandmother, who had come to visit from far away, let her wear a pink and clear crystal necklace with her recital dress, and her mother let her wear a special diamond and emerald ring! Seeing the beautiful ring on her finger while she was performing from memory was certainly different from looking at her bare hands. It was bound to deflect her concentration, but no one had thought of that.

An Emerging Self

Gradually, typical adolescent phases of the now twelve-year-old began to emerge. Here's one of the ways she became conscious of herself. In her diary, she wrote this:

> I wanted to be alone after the movie, alone in my room. Mom and her friend went to the kitchen for some iced tea. I left them and headed for bed, where I could gaze out at the star-filled night by my open window. Of course, after "Lassie Come Home," I wanted to think about my new love, Peter Lawford, and indulge my fantasies. Oh, to run in the sunny hills with Peter Lawford and Lassie! But something else was going on. Responding "No, thank you" to my mother's invitation to join her and Millie, I suddenly had a sense of my separateness and my difference. I just wanted to be me, alone, individual, and special. To her credit, my mom didn't press. I simply lay there in the dark looking at the stars and just being.

The recognition would come later that she had entered an awareness of herself in the classic adolescent state of being and growing. With the new awareness would come a certain amount of pride and independence along with its flip side—vulnerability, embarrassment, and a deep uneasiness about this new self.

Music? Playing the piano gradually became a frightening experience if she thought anyone were listening. A cloud of worry and anxiety, states of mind familiar to so many performers, followed her onto the stage. Fear of beginning again after a memory slip, worry that she would make a mistake or make the same mistake she had made the last time, dread of trying to explain herself to her teacher—all of these things distracted her and ensured anything but a successful and pleasurable performance experience.

Performance and Anxiety

In *Conscious Performing...from fear to freedom!*, Sally Bonkrude writes, "Performance is about relationship, connection, expression and an exchange of energy." By this definition, performance has many faces. Performance as interaction (public speaking, music performance, acting, sales presentations, etc.) requires an audience. The cultivation of shutting down the spontaneous expression of childhood, sometimes called "socialization," teaches conforming to the social norms required to make things run smoothly. This can run counter to spontaneous and expressive interaction.

Bonkrude points out that being free to express ourselves fully is authentic when we do not feel shut down. She speaks of an exchange of energy between performer and audience and describes what happens when anxiety enters the picture:

> *Performance anxiety happens when you move away from connecting with an authentic openness and, instead, close up and stop the energetic flow of connection between you and your audience.... Performance anxiety is an inability to be embodied and present with your audience...is anything that stops you from making an authentic, openhearted connection with your audience.* [1]

Further Developments

There was to be another recital, a partner recital shared with a violin student. The program would be lovely, with numbers alternating between piano and violin.

Though it went well, the recital was fraught with nerves. At twelve, she did not look forward to this performance in the same way that she had when she wore the yellow dress. She was worried that she wouldn't be ready.

Constantly with her was the fear of memory blackouts. She was always petrified, with a full-blown case of classic stage fright.

The evening of the recital arrived. Anxious and excited, she stepped out of the car, a princess in her recital dress. As usual, her mother had made it. It was a simple, long, white taffeta dress with a turquoise net overskirt that made it look as if shades of color were in the folds. Instead of sleeves, there were gathered net "wings" on the shoulders. She always loved special recital dresses. They made her feel beautiful, a little like playing "dress-up" when she was younger, but now, the real thing.

As she brushed past the marker post for cars to know where to stop at the edge of the grass, the lovely net overskirt caught on the post. A six-inch tear appeared at the bottom of the skirt. Her mother was furious! How could her daughter have been so careless?

A princess the moment before, the soon-to-be performer was ashamed and embarrassed for ruining her mother's laborious handiwork, and the happy mood of anticipation fell. But she had to play in a recital! Afraid she might begin to cry, she apologized to her mother, and they hoped together that the tear in the dress would not be noticed. She went into the University Library Recital Hall to perform at the piano. Nevertheless, her confidence, far from strong anyway, had been further shaken. As time went on, her memory of the occasion was not pleasurable; she thought of the recital with embarrassment. No compliments she had received had made any difference. Her own perception was that she could have played much better and, in fact, she could have.

The pleasure and sense of doing what she really wanted to do was fading away. There was some discussion with the teacher and her colleague, the former teacher, about motivation. She later remembered having asked for more dramatic pieces, ones that would help her express her feelings. Puzzled, the teacher and former teacher both listened and really tried to help. She was allowed to play a book of familiar symphonic themes arranged by Percy Grainger, as well as one or two teaching solos with considerable flair. The possibility of searching for satisfying music herself, though, was beyond her capability.

A general sense of shame was blooming like a weed. Her memorization was not secure. In utter humiliation, with clammy hands and a hot, blushing face, she felt ashamed that she finally had to take her music to the piano in another recital on the big stage instead of playing from memory. Each step she took toward the big, black, shiny piano was like lifting a lead brick with her foot. The instrument seemed alien, a monster she was asked to conquer, no longer her delightful friend. Her self-consciousness was at an all-time high., not so different, of course, from that of all adolescents.

Learning to Perform

In a university piano preparatory department in the 1940s, under the tutelage of well-educated college teachers, the little girl in the yellow dress did not have the benefit of educators' research into learning styles and processes that is available now. How can we teach students to perform today with poise and confidence? How can we be assured that they will enjoy sharing their music with listeners in an energetic exchange, as Bonkrude suggests, which is the true nature of performance?

After a student has learned a potential recital piece thoroughly, many aspects of performing itself can be taught and rehearsed. First of all, students can develop a constructive and humble attitude about what they are doing. They can think about what they want their music to convey—what they want their audiences to hear. They can learn to concentrate on the message in the music rather than on what the audience might think of them personally.

Making up stories for music can help, regardless of the student's age. Students of all ages can rehearse practical matters like going out on stage, taking bows, approaching the instrument (the piano, in this case), and resisting the urge to grimace when things don't go right. Grimaces tell the audience that the player has made a mistake. Most audiences, unaware that there is a problem, don't need to be distracted by their empathy for the poor soul who has played a wrong note or had to stop the music in humiliation.

Getting ready to perform can include playing through distractions (which the teacher can provide in rehearsal!), and most of all, keeping on going, no matter what. Students also can be reminded of the courtesy of saying "thank you" rather than explaining what they did not like about their performances ("I messed up.") when a listener compliments them later.

These are several "musts"—actions a student must do to prepare solid performances. They are the same, of course, as the ones we need to experience the thrill of excellence and accomplishment that is its own reward.

Memorizing

Solid steps in memorizing should include learning to start at section changes and phrase beginnings. This way, a performer can always jump ahead to the next "landmark" to keep on going if there's an unexpected stumble or a memory gap. It is critical to notice the similarities and differences between appearances of motives to avoid confusion. Special attention can be given to memorizing the beginning and ending (getaways!).

A performer can always conclude a piece gracefully if he or she knows securely how it ends!

Recovering from memory slips, like knowing every aspect of the music based on this detailed analysis so performance can continue without interruption, was not discussed, much less rehearsed, in early lessons for the little girl in the yellow dress. But the "just in case" strategies add to confidence in recitals, competitions, and auditions. They are rarely needed, most likely because they foster a very thorough understanding of the structure of the music.

Lots of attention should be given to training the muscular mechanism because playing an instrument is intensely physical. Very slow practice on small and sometimes awkward passages, and the opposite—playing a figure with totally relaxed and spontaneous effort—are important. One of the most difficult steps is not playing at all, but imagining oneself playing—"thinking" a piece away from the instrument, recalling each note and gesture. Effective practicing, as described earlier, makes memorizing much easier.

Improvising

Improvisation was not taught in classical lessons, and the little girl was too cautious and unadventurous to make up her own music. But improvisation and composition might have helped round out her comprehension of the music. If the little girl had been asked to make up her own pieces, she might have enjoyed imagining a composer's compositional process herself. As a result, she might have found her pieces much easier to understand.

It was fascinating to me as a teacher to notice that students' compositions quite often reflected the styles of pieces they were studying. They had *absorbed* the idiomatic gestures of the composers and successfully imitated them!

If we assume that when a student has memorized a piece and can play it consistently well in the studio he or she is ready to play for an audience

— this is the part where the student gets held out over the abyss (see the Preface)—we have stopped short of testing the student's real knowledge. What to do when things don't go the way we have expected? It is ideal if students can draw on that assurance that they really know what they are doing, what the music is made of.

A student who can improvise is in good territory here. I once listened in fascination as my student played the third movement of the Ginastera Sonata op. 22, no. 1, on a public recital and improvised his way through a long section he had forgotten. Aside from obvious flaws in his preparation, no one knew the difference, or at least it didn't matter, because it was so stylistically appropriate! He maintained his poise. The audience's spell of involvement was not broken. This skill doesn't have to be limited to professionals.

Recovering

In another example of recovery, of overcoming a memory slip or a wrong note, a student was performing the first movement of the Mozart Sonata, K. 332, and found herself repeating the entire first part of the piece as she moved into the end. She lost her concentration and missed the "gate" to the Recapitulation, that repeated or similar passage which, instead of changing to a new key as it had in the Exposition, heralds a conclusion by remaining in the home key. In front of an audience of 125, she calculated, without hesitating or missing a beat, that she could end the piece at the conclusion of the Exposition, even though she knew it would be in the wrong key for the ending. As her teacher, I gasped, afraid she'd play the whole thing again. But she was right—only her classmates heard the difference, and they looked at each other in puzzlement. She came off the stage grinning as our eyes met, and I was clapping extra loudly. (This young lady went on to become a performance major with a master's degree.)

Students need to think of performing as acting. "It's as if you are an actor on stage," I would say. "You wouldn't stop and say to the audience that you'd like to say that line again because you forgot some of it." That always evoked laughter because all school-age students have been in plays and skits and can see the absurdity. We practiced keeping on going, not letting the audience know you didn't like the way a passage sounded, not breaking the "bubble" of listening by letting your personal dismay get in the way. "It's not about you—it's about sharing beautiful music with the audience" was one of the mantras I repeated with young pianists. This seemed to increase the poise and assuage their anxiety about performing, at least in part. Performance of music is sharing, presenting a nonverbal gift to listeners. Performers are often thought of as entertainers. Not so. In the performance of classical music, they are vehicles or conduits through which musical messages travel.

Preparing for Style

With the hundreds of teaching pieces that have been written these days for masterwork style preparation, young students have an opportunity to play with drama and flair. Because some of these pieces often have an abundance of patterns adapted from various styles that are easy to recognize, they are also easy to memorize. These are, as pedagogue Louise Bianchi used to say, "pupil savers," and can give the student an important sense of command and power to make the instrument "sing." The young performer engages the music more easily, and that energetic communication with the listener soon takes place, simply delighting everybody.

Searching for this kind of repertoire requires preparatory time on the teacher's part, browsing in a music store, perusing a catalog, or attending conferences at which workshops and showcases of new music are presented.

All these forms of preparation for performance can be summed up humorously. My students and I asked how we could organize the butterflies that flutter in the stomach during performance so that the red ones were all together, the black ones, the striped ones, etc. This image was fun for students of all ages!

⁓

Haunted

The young teenage student's ratings in National Guild Auditions began to slip. It seemed to her that her peers played much better than she did. As motivation to do well faded, no one asked if something were wrong or if she were no longer interested in music. Soon, practicing dwindled to almost nothing. She had been responsible for registering herself for lessons each year at the university. Her parents had said she should stop because she wasn't practicing enough. She believed them. Later, they were surprised that she had indeed not signed up. She had studied piano for five years.

Then, another move came when she was fifteen. Her father had been working in the small town for six years. Moving to a new teaching job in another town was not out of the ordinary for college faculty. Bigger town, bigger college, and, one would assume, a better salary. This time, there was no discussion about finding another piano teacher. She was beginning her senior year in high school. With only one more year of school and possibly a year of work before college (because she would be only sixteen when she graduated), it seemed pointless, even though she did ask for lessons. The family was busy, and she was the youngest. No wonder no one remembered her asking. Piano was not important anymore. Besides, nowhere in her memory had her father or her siblings attended recitals during the piano study years unless they, too, were taking lessons. In the new house she played the piano regularly, took on new pieces from the music at hand, both her mother's music and her own, and tried to tackle pieces that were really too difficult, again simply playing only the more accessible passages. It was then that the toxic weed of shame developed into the attitude that there would always be some part of every classical piece that she would have to try to "get away with," that was unpredictable and a block to playing competently. Music certainly stayed with her, however.

Her mother said she could always tell her mood by what she played and the way she played it. But her mother seemed always to find something for her to do when she played the piano. Help with supper, feed the dog, straighten up her room. (Of course, she usually played at an inopportune time—when those requests were likely to come up!). She often made music when she was waiting to go out or for a friend to arrive. She played for Sunday School and at her friends' houses, though she didn't memorize or perform.

In a gap year of working before college, she bought a 45-rpm record player with her first paycheck and began to collect classical records. At the family's former home there were some old, breakable records and a windup Victrola in the hallway. When they had moved to the new town, these things had been discarded. Her father was disgusted that she had spent the first money she made on "frivolity." He was probably afraid that she would become a spendthrift. In his mind, the family once had the means of playing recordings, the Victrola had been discarded with the last move, and the need for it had passed. The first record album she purchased was a collection of short classics on four small, red, plastic discs that would automatically drop down one by one from a six-inch-tall cylinder at the appropriate times. Beethoven's Eroica *Symphony soon followed, a gift from her brother, suggested by her mother.*

Support from an Unexpected Source

Auntie always listened. Her father's aunt had lived with the family almost from the beginning of the young pianist's life. She was legally blind and a recluse. She read letters and newspapers with a magnifying glass as much as she could, listened daily to news and Major League Baseball games on her beloved radio, and kept to her room most of the time. She was sarcastic and blunt and rejected the overtures of the family's friends.

She had come with the family to Texas in 1937 and kept up with her friends in Philadelphia through correspondence. On hot days, she treated the family, even the dog, to ice cream cones at the corner drugstore. Packages came for her from the East on special occasions. The dog alerted everyone that they contained Whitman's chocolates. Auntie complained that she didn't like the dog, but somehow he knew that she was worth a bite-sized bonbon or two.

Auntie outlived her friends, and lived, herself, to the remarkable age of ninety-three. She and her niece didn't get along well. As a "grand dame," she irritated the girl's mother. Pushing her empty coffee cup toward her hostess, who controlled the coffee pot at breakfast, she would say, "If you please."

But Auntie listened. When the adolescent musician played the piano in the small house the family lived in after the last move, she turned off her radio without complaint. It didn't matter how many mistakes she heard or how poorly the music was played. Her gesture gave the young girl a clear message, which caused her to think, "I'll practice this piece for Auntie—I know she likes it."

What Is "Support"?

Many times, support is manifested simply as interest by one person or a family for another's efforts. Other times, it is being invited to play in a special recital, an individual audition, or competition opportunity offered by the studio or a school that helps a student grow. I found that my confidence in a student's readiness to participate in music events was, in a subtle way, a vote of support. On the other hand, from time to time, we needed a heart-to-heart talk to acknowledge that the student's preparation had not been enough, for whatever reason, and that it would be best to forego an opportunity rather than risk having an embarrassing, disastrous experience. It's simply not necessary to place students in situations that could quite possibly be extremely disappointing for them. As Louise Bianchi often said in pedagogy class, "We must arrange for success."

It doesn't take much for children to feel supported in their activities, and the support doesn't have to be dramatic. Praise, or "positive reinforcement," has reached its zenith today, when parents exclaim "Good job!" for the least gesture of ordinary accomplishment by their children (like picking up a piece of trash). Even music teachers say, "Well done!" or "Gooood!" when something really isn't. Children know when they have done well and will soon discount gushing compliments that don't fit. There almost always is, however, something a teacher likes and can mention, then move on to discussing how to play something even better. My students were so familiar with that routine that one regularly teased me, saying "Now…" when I had finished with the compliments!

Some students, however, are so accustomed to having their parents praise whatever they play that they find a teacher's suggestion, no matter how tactfully presented, an affront. These students are living in a house of cards in which they know at some level that they are not being dealt with truthfully. Often the one-on-one relationship with a teacher exacerbates this situation. I had a student once who became quite rude if I corrected, tactfully, a mistake in her playing. Finally, I asked her about her feelings, whether or not she felt that way at school if she didn't understand something. Her response: "Well, at school I have time to fix it." She could observe and self-correct before she "went public."

On the other hand, early in my teaching, I observed that a highly gifted young student could not accept any praise I offered. After reading an article about gifted students in a professional journal, I tried redirecting the praise away from the *person* of the student and toward the music. I put my always-held pencil down, moved my chair back, relaxed my position, and asked him to play the piece again just so I could enjoy it. He was smart enough, maybe not even consciously, to realize that he had played so well that I simply wanted to enjoy the music and not be a "teacher" for the moment. We could then talk about what worked and what he could do even better.

In my studio, a form of peer support came from the camaraderie of several students' having been to music camp together, or participating in an event with students of other studios, a larger venue than regular studio recitals. Weekly group lessons helped. They included much more than performance—theory games, shared problems of memorizing, teaching each other their most difficult memory passages as a means of sharpening their own observations about the passage, studying fingering issues together, learning to listen by humanely critiquing each other's work and, on special occasions, studying other arts for elements that all arts have in common. Today I would add biography and music history as much as possible.

⟋⟍

Another source of genuine support for the little girl came from relatives she wasn't able to see very often.

The children in this family seldom saw their only living grandparents, whose home was far away, but there were weekly letters to the children's parents and, many times, special letters for the youngsters. It was taken for granted that the use of long-distance telephone was for emergencies or urgent news that couldn't wait for the mail, even air mail, and not for chatting or catching up on activities. Yet the three children had a close relationship with their mother's parents, from whom they had lived just up the street in their earliest years.

Every so often, these grandparents, who traveled annually even during World War II, came to visit for a few days if their trip had taken them on a reasonably close route. Their suitcases smelled of fine pipe tobacco and exquisite perfume and held special surprises—dolls and jewelry from Mexico or exotic countries in South America. They showed amateur movies of foreign cultures and told stories for hours. But the grandmother always had time to ask the resident pianist to play for her. And when the young pianist was able, once or twice, to visit the grandparents' home in Philadelphia, she learned that the piano tuner had just been there.

She accompanied her mother to Philadelphia to celebrate the grandparents' fiftieth wedding anniversary with a big dinner at a fine hotel ballroom. When her grandmother asked her to perform at this momentous occasion, she agreed reluctantly. Nevertheless, she prepared Schumann's "Träumerei," one of her special recital pieces, to play for the large audience. She knew she had played well when she received many compliments from the guests, especially from her dear grandparents, about her expressive performance. Her dread ahead of time was a small price to pay for knowing that she had contributed to the celebration in such a special way.

Ready to Leave Home

Eventually she left for college, packing those Schirmer editions of the classics in her belongings. She found the practice rooms in the catacombs of the old music building on the campus and diligently headed over there daily at 6:30 a.m. to practice before breakfast. She set no goals and received no direction or support from any source. Inevitably, academics and a part-time job won out in the competition for her time, and she stopped, limiting her piano playing to visits home.

Along with the baggage she took to college was a well-established overlay of subtle, unidentified shame and the assumption that while she would do well enough, she would always fall short of what was expected of her.

But college was a happy experience. Complain, complain! "Oh, my gosh, I have to write another paper for English this week!" Nevertheless, she loved it and decided to major in English. Combining that with philosophy and history as minors seemed a perfect fit. Her father was disappointed that she wasn't more interested in science like he was. "You can't eat English," he said. From his perspective, the only reason for women to be educated was to prepare themselves to work in case they didn't marry or something fatal happened to their husbands. "He must be right," she said to herself. "I'd better add an education course, like he suggested. That way I'll have 'insurance.'" Three weeks later, thoroughly disinterested, she dropped it for Introductory Philosophy. She realized later that her father certainly valued educating oneself to grow intellectually for its own sake, despite his view that women's main job was to help men.

The college environment provided many cultural opportunities. Special plays, lectures, and concerts were held on campus. A fine music school was part of the university. The young student attended symphonies and recitals frequently, taking advantage of special tickets or ushering to earn free admission. She wondered, "Why do I always want to cry at piano concerts?"

Maybe they reminded her of how much she had enjoyed making music.

Maybe they made her vaguely ashamed of stopping her music study.

The most satisfying experiences were visiting her friend's practice room, sitting on the floor just to listen while she practiced. Often when others played, she wanted to take their places at the keyboard. Her friend's musical expressiveness, however, was unique in that it felt fulfilling for her as a listener.

But the long hiatus had begun. She didn't play the piano for fifteen years.

III

Cultivation

Connecting Dots

Mid-Century

In the decade of the fifties, it was more the rule than the exception that college women married before graduating and either went to work to support their husbands' education or worked and went to school simultaneously. Betty Friedan's *The Feminine Mystique,* published in 1963, spoke to the dilemma of the well-educated housewife feeling marooned with small children, unable to continue her formal studies and with nowhere to apply her academic expertise. To the extent that she could satisfy her well-trained intellectual curiosity on her own behalf, she was quite possibly a calmer and more competent mother and more likely to enjoy her young children.

Unfoldings

Life for the college graduate and now grown musician moved on with marriage and the arrival of children.

Offering to take care of the children for a few days, her mother provided her with a little time off from her responsibilities. She happily visited friends in another city. At an old friend's home, she had a chance to play the piano again. The only available music was a hymnal. Because she thought she didn't know how to improvise, she was happy enough simply to add octaves to some of her favorite hymns. But a surprising message to herself came through clearly: "I must find a way to have a piano of my own."

Asking her mother for the old elephant piano had gotten her nowhere. Besides, moving it to where she lived two-hundred-fifty miles away would have been nearly impossible and certainly too costly. She lived in a small rural community, and because no one in the nearby little church knew even as much music as she did, she directed the choir of six and played for congregational singing. Slipping over to the church, she played the piano as often as she could when her children were under someone else's care. After all, she had those Schirmer editions—the Bach Inventions, some Beethoven and Mozart Sonatas, as well as miscellaneous Chopin and Schubert pieces. Practicing and playing the piano again reminded her that she had never ceased to love music, especially making music herself at the piano.

Libraries

As a music teacher, I could not guess which young students would play their instruments as adults, from the least promising to the most interested ones. Just in case they would return to playing long after they had dropped formal lessons, I thought it would be worthwhile for them to have developed their own collection of printed music, no matter how simple. One of the legacies of the early piano training in the life of the little girl in the yellow dress was the accumulation of a valuable library.

As an adjudicator of festivals, auditions, and competitions today, I frequently see that music presented by a student is from a teacher's library, issued on loan to students as they are ready for it, and is even, on rare occasions these days, illegally photocopied. I certainly appreciate teachers' wanting to help students' families save money, even their fear that willing and eager students might not be able to continue with lessons if music costs were prohibitive. (It's ironic that the more successful a student is, the more the need exists to acquire or purchase new music.)

Each teacher of school-age students needs to work this problem out, to be sure, but in my view, the building of a library can be critical. I am convinced that my return to the piano was possible when it happened because I had good music at home, available to me right away. I'm not sure I would have ventured out to find a music store where I could buy it, much less felt justified in spending money from a lean household budget on an endeavor for myself when the outcome was uncertain.

I believe it is valuable to help a student build a music library from the very beginning. Even while he or she is advancing in the studio, a great deal of pleasure might be found in going back over earlier material long forgotten. (Think of the sight reading opportunities here from books in which just a few pieces were learned!) And having good editions selected by a teacher will be a treasure to have on hand later. We can assume that the teacher is a better judge of which editions will be enduring, granted that new editions are published constantly.

Few adults who return to making music would head for a music store right away. They might, instead, find old books in their accumulated libraries to be extremely helpful. Even the earliest music for the beginning student might be valuable for one who returns to practice and has forgotten much. The teacher may have marked on the music special reminders or alterations in fingering that were unique to the student.

Always Present

Music had always been there for our musician. In the years she wasn't playing the piano, she began to write poetry, unaware that it was a creative outlet and that some of it reflected music. In the following poems she wrote is evidence of her tussle with the joy and angst music created in her:

Affirmation	Interruption
Bach takes your life	To lay aside my book
And lays it in sequence	All interest lost
Before you	To the compelling strains
Makes you feel	Of music's voice
Pain of loss	To close my eyes, then
Of hurt	Grateful for the sound
Almost forgotten	
	And feel poetry
And then	Spill forth from
Reminds you	A full heart
That such belongs to	
What brought you	Is to be alive
To this moment of listening	

Then, finally, a piano in her house! It was after a move to the city. She had made a commitment to herself—if she had to sell some heirloom jewelry to get it, she would find a way to buy a piano. Ever since that visit to old friends, when she'd had a chance to begin playing again, it was as if a little voice deep inside kept saying, "You must play again. You must find a way to have a piano and play it whenever you can." Sometimes, as if by providence, people provide one with amazing opportunities, like opening doors, at critical times in life. Over coffee one day, she asked an older friend to whom she often went for advice, "Do you know how to sell a valuable antique ring?" Her friend wondered why she would want to do that but suggested a place to start. When she learned that the plan was to buy a piano, the friend said, "Oh, don't sell your ring. Let's just move my daughter's piano over to your house; she won't need it 'til she's out of college two years from now." So, on a borrowed piano moved ten blocks in a pickup truck, she began to practice regularly and gradually to regain keyboard skill. That was the value, after all, of having collected a music library when she was young. The music was at hand.

A piano in her living room! A studio upright, it had been painted dark green. She thought it was absolutely wonderful. She got up in the middle of the night to see it again and convince herself it was really there. Her husband traveled often, and after the children went to bed, she began to practice regularly at night. She wanted her three young children to have an appetite for music, so she pledged to herself that she would not keep them from the piano by trying to practice with concentration when they were around. Instead, they played and sang together, and she did her serious work, learning, analyzing, and memorizing at night, after their bedtime. Out of the box again came the G. Schirmer classics!

If only she could take lessons again. Here she was, only several months after the piano-on-loan had arrived, feeling the need for help. One day, an old friend who had been a piano teacher for twenty years arrived in town. This wonderful friend agreed to take the hungry student on. It was as if another door had been opened. The date for her first lesson approached. She couldn't sleep, her stomach was upset, and her palms were cold and clammy that day! It mattered that much. The questions popped up: "What if she thinks I'm wasting my time? Will she want to stick with me?" She found herself sitting at the teacher's Steinway upright being introduced to a Bach Prelude and accepting an assignment to practice several pieces before the next lesson. Her teacher was patient and kind, and the once-again student began to relax, hardly able to believe she was actually taking lessons again.

She knew that, for her, music needed to be shared. Playing only for herself was just not enough. The communication of feelings expressed by good music required interaction with other humans. She had never dreamed of becoming a music teacher, but there it was.

Later she shuddered to think of how unprepared she had been to begin teaching. She asked her teacher friend to help. The teacher, recognizing the situation, gave her advice. After schooling her student in curriculum resources and techniques of pedagogy, she "looked over her shoulder" and periodically listened to the new teacher's handful of students—the first five—play. She encouraged this beginning teacher all the way. Our musician had begun a babysitting exchange, trading lesson tuition for a friend's two children for care of her own children during the lessons. By the time five years had passed, she had established a home studio. She was vaguely embarrassed, though, and felt like an imposter without credentials. She did not have the nerve to find a music teachers' group in which she could learn new ideas, participate in workshops, and experience collegiality. She said to herself, "How dare I teach young students when I've had no more than five years of piano lessons as a child and a few as an adult! What if somebody who is a 'real' teacher finds out?"

As for performing, she worked up pieces to play for indulgent friends who loved whatever she could play. She eventually had a studio of fifteen and bought a piano of her own! Shopping for her used Gulbransen studio model was a thrill. It was trim and brown and had been well cared for, with regular tuning. The salesman said he enjoyed selling her this instrument so much more than even a new grand to someone who just wanted to put it in a bay window and didn't even need to hear how it sounded.

Back to School

Another move came for the young family, back to the city where she had gone to college. She discovered that another old friend was in the right place at the right time. Another door began to open. She had known this friend fourteen years earlier; she had frequented the friend's practice room at the college. This friend also had returned to that campus and was studying for a master's degree in piano performance just for that year. The new teacher began taking lessons from this graduate student in exchange for teaching one of her children.

Realizing her friend would not be available after that year of graduate study, this newcomer discussed with her family the idea of taking lessons again for herself at the university. Then she asked her graduate student friend, "Do you think they would accept me as a piano student?"

The friend answered, "Of course. Let's pick out the repertoire you will need to play for an audition."

The family thought it was a good idea, and so did the teacher/friend.

The first back-to-school experience was a year of lessons. There it was again just before the first lesson—the fear, the anxiety. What was she doing? Sweaty, clammy, cold hands, an upset stomach, and a sleepless night. These nervous symptoms seemed to indicate either that she shouldn't be doing this or the opposite—that taking lessons at the university was so important that she was finally on the right path. Time would tell.

Within a year, she bought an old but stable grand piano to keep her Gulbransen studio model company and acquired enough students to establish a small studio. Two of her own children were part of it. She managed to incorporate their lessons into the busy after-school schedule. Her teacher at the university suggested that she think about entering a degree plan. Her first reaction was negative—"Not enough money and not enough time. Impossible!"

But for the next ten years, she took courses and piano lessons on a degree plan.

The university was only three miles away. She practiced there after classes. Progress was slow but steady. As the studio grew, she hurried home for the first lessons in the early afternoon. The living/dining room "L" space became filled with pianos, book shelves, a chalkboard, a table for group work, and a pleasant waiting area in the corner. Luckily, a family room had been adapted from an enclosed porch on the other side of the kitchen, making it possible for the studio to be contained without having to be converted to a family space in off hours.

But performances still terrified her. The semester's end juries became worse and worse. (The fact that they were called "juries" didn't help.) Constantly, she questioned her decision to pursue music. She could have, instead, applied for a master's program in English literature! "What is the matter with me?" she often asked herself.

She was appalled to discover what she didn't know. Having taught her own children, she was dismayed to realize what she had left out. She did, at least, know that she had passed along her love of music to all of her students, but oh, how deprived they had been of certain technical and theoretical knowledge!

She spent long hours at the piano but didn't really know how to practice. Her required junior degree recital was probational. Later she enjoyed the humor supplied by her supportive fellow students when she ended the arpeggio at the conclusion of the "Gigue," in the Bach Partita 1, BWV 825, on the 7th. Her friends said, "It's a good thing you had to play a repeat!" They knew she would have another chance to get it right, by playing the indicated repeat on the score, to end the piece on the correct (tonic) note. No one would notice the error that way!

She learned more from friends who were twenty years younger than she did from her piano teachers. She was reasonably mature and articulate, though, and had a million questions. Her teachers liked to talk to her, and she enjoyed the respite from the lessons. For her, it was an avoidance mechanism, and for them, it was a chance to play, to show her how it was done. That was, after all, still the traditional way to teach, by demonstration and example.

Although she didn't realize it yet, in retrospect this seemed to be another subtle experience of not being taken seriously, much like her experience of feeling that her family had not supported her. Taking her seriously would have meant probing thoroughly to discover what she knew and didn't know, where the obvious holes were in her background, and addressing them. Perhaps that would have helped assuage the intensity of the fear of being grossly inadequate for the job.

Grateful later that she had even been accepted into the music department at all, she remembered that these teachers, even in the seventies, were simply using traditional approaches to teaching at the college level. They assumed that students had developed good work habits by the time they had entered college.

A semester's end piano exam illustrated the point. An atmosphere of sympathetic condescension surrounded the jury of four gentlemen. In her vivid dream the night before, the piano bench was moving from side to side, and the keyboard was floating just out of her grasp. In real life, she entered the jury studio as if to an execution. Soon, she skipped an entire page in her Debussy piece with a terrifying memory slip and stopped for a few seconds, trying to recall her place in the music. Just behind her elbow sat one professor, who said, "You want an F sharp there," puncturing her feeble concentration as she tried vainly to figure out where he meant. Afterward, the spokesman for the group said, "My dear, it's as if the sword of Damocles hangs over your head. Why don't you change your major to piano pedagogy?" As it was then, pedagogy was considered to be a stepchild. Real musicians majored in their chosen instrument. Later she challenged her teacher: "Unless you tell me I am completely in the wrong field, I want to keep on." He did not have the courage to tell her to back off. Thank goodness! On the other hand, neither did he have the insight to suggest alternative routes toward accomplishing her goal of getting a degree in piano.

In today's world, forty-odd years later, students who want to be performance majors are much more carefully screened. The young woman's performance issues would have sent up a prohibitive red flag, perhaps calling for some serious remedial work. Nevertheless, the degree was completed, finally, and with the considerable help of some young friends, the senior recital was quite successful. She had earned a double major: piano performance and piano pedagogy.

She kept right on taking lessons after graduation. It had been a high-wire act from which she dared not look down, managing a home with three teenage children, facing a dissolving marriage, teaching in her home studio, and practicing all at the same time. Overriding it all was her constant thought that went something like, "Excuse me while I try to learn to play the piano."

She loved school, though, and there were many answers to the questions she'd had for a long time. She was able to apply her pedagogy studies immediately in her home studio. Courses in repertoire, group dynamics, and theory were what she had needed and hungered for. She had learned so much; she didn't care how long it had taken.

Becoming a "Real" Teacher

As a single mom by this time, she expanded her teaching studio as much as she could and took a second part-time job for the next three years to make ends meet.

She worked to make her studio more professional, organizing policies, materials, and routines. She began teaching regular group lessons in addition to private ones on a weekly basis, continuing the model that her pedagogy professors had developed. One teacher had willingly accepted reports from her group lessons as part of lab work for one of the courses.

She pondered buying a brand-new Baldwin grand piano, knowing she would have to finance it. She could imagine her father saying it would be self-indulgent. Once she saw it as a business machine, though, the doubts went away quickly!

Adding such a fine instrument to the studio changed students' attitudes in a subtle way. As if it were speaking of taking things seriously, the studio seemed to say to the students, "What we are doing here is really special." Once a fifth-grade student shared with her a paper she had written for school about one of her favorite places. She described the piano studio as a place that, in a good way, "just feels like working."

She joined the local music teachers association and got to know her colleagues, becoming good friends with several teachers who warmly gave her advice about student events and repertoire when she needed it. She constantly learned new ideas and new repertoire from excellent monthly programs and workshops on new teaching materials. This path continued for some time as she concentrated on becoming a better teacher and found happiness in a new marriage.

Still, she found herself saying to people who inquired about her piano background, "Perform? Me? No, I don't play in public. But my students do. Be sure to come to our recital next Sunday afternoon."

She taught her students how to perform, though, including what to do if things didn't go the way they had intended. They seemed to love recitals. Sometimes the less self-conscious younger ones bounded off the one-foot-high stage at the end of their performances with delight in their experiences, feeling that they had communicated especially well. One student's father, a psychotherapist, commented that it was clear that the students felt "empowered." She mused that one learns to teach best what was most difficult for oneself. Perhaps she was becoming the kind of teacher she might have wished for herself.

As for her own performing, she played constantly at the second piano with her students without worrying about it. At studio recitals, though, when she played a second piano accompaniment with more and more advanced students, that old bugaboo about being inadequate sat on the bench beside her.

In another city, she found the teacher for herself whom she had always needed. She managed to study continuously for some time, practicing diligently as she finally began to learn how to go about it herself. She enjoyed sharing with her students the same practice challenges they were encountering in their own work. They were nearly always surprised to learn that she was taking lessons. In a subtle way, they were learning about lifetime study—a good thing.

But a pattern began to emerge as she tried hard to please the new teacher. Shame and anxiety were still hovering like vultures, waiting for her to give up. It was a subtle condition, this common "stage fright" that performers love to talk about. As she went from wild enthusiasm and thrill with the repertoire and interpretive insights suggested by the new teacher to horrible lessons filled with nerves and disastrous playing, she said to herself, "Hey, I've been through this before."

Here's the pattern: Someone, a teacher, seems quite supportive and interested in teaching her, based on something heard in her playing. To her this interest and support are a supreme compliment because she is in awe of the teacher, who plays exquisitely and professionally. "How could someone like that want to teach me?" Then the feeling of not deserving such attention, the fear of displeasing the authority, the hopelessness about ever doing it right, sets in. Lessons become embarrassing ordeals. "Surely he will tell me soon he doesn't want to teach me anymore." Old tapes play—"Who do you think you are?" When her mother learned that her daughter's new teacher was a concert artist, she asked, "Does he give you a real lesson?" As it turned out, she learned a great deal from this new postgraduate teacher, and a lot about teaching, as they became friends and worked through many of her performance issues.

Once, some time later, she consulted a psychotherapist to work on problems with anger, even rage. Before long, they arrived at the topic of performance anxiety. One of his strategies in working with her was having her reenact performing for the teacher at different stages in her early piano studies. She played pieces appropriate for different ages in her development, then moved to the teacher's chair to pick up the role of instructor, and back and forth.

In the teacher's chair, she spoke gently with the imaginary student, asking lots of questions about what the student thought of this or that musical passage, what the composer might say if he were here to explain the piece, how best to practice a certain section. She asked questions that would help the student discover repeating patterns, changing dynamics, where else in the score the piece might have ended appropriately, whether there was a special ending, or coda. It was all about discovering the subtleties of the music and planning how to learn it.

The therapist said, "You have become the teacher you didn't have."

IV

Taproot

Finding Answers

Shame Emerges

John Bradshaw, in *Healing the Shame That Binds You*, says this about shame:

> In itself, shame is not bad. Shame is a normal human emotion.
>
> In fact, it is necessary to have the feeling of shame if one is to be truly human.... Shame tells us of our limits. Shame keeps us in our human boundaries, letting us know we can and will make mistakes, and that we need help.... Healthy shame is the psychological foundation of humility.[1]

She still had not solved the nagging issue of shame as a pervasive theme in her life. Where had it come from? She had not yet associated it with the fear of piano performance. Nor the anger, the underlying rage that, while she experienced it less and less as she matured, she still recognized and remembered in her original family.

Finding a Treasure

The photograph albums and letters gave her insights that later would help put shape to her story. They came into her possession fortuitously. Helping her mother clear out her father's things after his death a year or so earlier, she had, with her mother's reluctant permission, packed up the albums of pictures to take home and peruse at a later date. Her mother's household helper had moved things out of the old bureau, so tall that she had considered seeing the top as a milestone during her growing childhood. The albums had been left in a drawer, even though the mother's instructions had been to throw them away. The housekeeper had persuaded the widowed mother that her daughter might like to see them, and they shouldn't be discarded for a while. She had opened the musty drawer to find two crumbling albums of black and white snapshots fastened onto the pages with black slip-in corners.

She held the albums in her lap at the airport the day she left her mother's house to return to her home in another city. Now they were wrapped in clinging plastic to contain their crumbling contents. Looking at the yellowing pictures, she had been astounded! "Why have I not seen these before?" she pondered. True, she was the youngest child by five years, and quite possibly by the time she was old enough to remember them, the rest of the family had forgotten them. That was the point. Everything about her father's family was remote. Her own family had moved from a big eastern city around the end of the Great Depression to the Southwest, where her father was lucky to find work at all. The pictures of him in his boyhood and early adulthood were not important, though, and were not part of the family lore—not for her as the youngest child, anyway.

Her mother expressed some hesitation about letting her have the albums. As she sat beside her mother, waiting for the plane, she noticed that her mother seemed uncomfortable. Suddenly, it dawned on her that her mother felt ashamed of her husband's family. The loyal daughter promised to take good care of the photos and to return them promptly if they were wanted. Soon after arriving home, she wrote a long letter suggesting that her dad had been ashamed of his family and that her mother had assimilated that feeling.

Dear Mom…

…the power of the shame in Dad's family that hung like a cloud over relationships, decisions, and so on…. You were a dutiful wife protecting Dad's family pride; indeed, the shame was your shame, too…. The shame is the big insight for me. It was passed on to Dad, to you, to us on many occasions and in many ways, like a poison…. We never saw the photos that Dad couldn't quite throw away. We heard little about his childhood—we didn't see the portraits of his parents. It was better to let things lie and get on with it. I can see that it must have seemed wise. But I picked it up anyway. Something dark about Daddy's family.

Her mother responded immediately with appreciation for her daughter's perception and understanding. She didn't need the photos returned after all.

Not telling this youngest of three children much about her paternal grand-family was easy because they had died when this youngest was a baby, and she hadn't known them at all. The children heard instead about their other grandfamily and had come to know them with deep affection.

The two albums were fascinating. Looking at them marked the beginning of our now-adult musician's long period of "catching on." The photographs dated back to her father's boyhood in the teens of the twentieth century. The fragile black paper with its variety of snapshots showed a family of some means (probably at the first acquisition of a camera).

Then there was the family at home. Before the first car, there was a carriage with a horse at the tall Philadelphia house. The ladies wore nice, fashion-ably long, and sometimes ruffled dresses with bustles. They were turn o' the century (twentieth) clothes. Hats had feathers and frills. The men could only be described, more than one hundred years later, as "dapper." Hair parted in the middle, handlebar moustaches.

As she looked, as if moving into the pictures themselves, the questions bubbled up. Why had she never seen these? Was it really that, because she was the youngest, no one thought to show them to her after the family had looked at them when she was too young to remember? Was it as simple as that? Or was it her dad's embarrassment about his family? Was that real or imagined? She had no way to be sure.

Yet little things kept emerging, like pieces of a puzzle floating just beyond her vision.

There were the three little boys, of whom her father was the middle, all dressed up like miniature adults, posing for the camera on special days. Although she had not seen these pictures, she had known that both of these grandparents were born in the United States to German immigrant couples. She had known of the daughter who died so young because she had seen her in a lovely large pastel portrait that had been in her family's possession as far back as she could remember.

The two albums covered quite a span of time. This granddaughter imagined the family's supporting business, a classic local ice cream and cake parlor, to be a community gathering place in Philadelphia before World War I.

From talking with her mother toward the end of her mother's life, she was reminded of her paternal grandmother's losses and the way the grandmother placed a heavy obligation on her middle son, the musician's father. There was definitely a thread of family shame coming down through generations. She could sense it, even see it, but she still hadn't put things together.

Acquiring the box of family letters came later, when she helped pack up her aging mother for a move to a retirement center. Hauled home, it sat unexamined in the closet for nearly ten years. Finally, it demanded attention and brought her to a point of connecting the dots between family issues and her musical development.

All of the ingredients for family shame were present, including bankruptcy, partly due to mismanagement but also due to changing times leading up to the Great War. These devout and religious people could only assume guilt for the way their lives were unfolding and think that the punishment of a Victorian god was clearly behind their travails.

Generations

In exploring work that has been written about shame in families, I came across the insights of Edwin H. Friedman, who wrote, in *Generation to Generation,* of family systems, or processes. A major theme of his work is the significance of the family of origin, along with its web of relatives and special friends, as an extended family field for functioning in the present. A family system is a network that can be either debilitating or enabling/healing. Although this may seem obvious, or a matter of common sense, it has been studied systematically only since about 1980.

Friedman said that patterns of behavior and reactions to episodes in one's life can be seen to repeat from one generation to another. Emotional processes are at work in individual families and the influence of previous generations can be seen in lifecycle events. In the case of illness, such as alcoholism or depression, this is most dramatic. Understanding family networks and their convolutions may be commonplace today, but my study to understand how these things work has helped me to allow more subtle manifestations of certain patterns to heal. Friedman talks about overcoming family issues:

> *Gaining a better understanding of the emotional processes still at work with regard to our family of origin, and modifying our response to them, can aid significantly in the resolution of emotional problems in our immediate family.... In addition, specific patterns of behavior, perceptions, and thinking...have an uncanny way of reappearing.*

When family members are able to see beyond the horizons of their own nuclear family area of trouble and observe the transmission of such issues from generation to generation, they can obtain more distance from their immediate problems, and, as a result, become freer to make changes.[2]

The Past as Destiny

As Susan Griffin said in *Wrestling with the Angels of Democracy,* children always long to know the truth, whatever it is:

The proverb promising that the sins of the fathers will be visited on the next generation has many levels of meaning. Justice has a secret life among children. An injustice committed by her parents or grandparents can lodge in a child's mind, even if the child knows nothing of the events and all that she feels is a kind of emptiness somewhere in her soul, coupled, at times, with an unexplained longing.[3]

Because children always want to know what's real (the truth), they *will* know it emotionally. There is no way to keep them from knowing it at the emotional level, which is certainly not to say they are aware of their knowing. Many times, what children are told is not congruent with what they see and feel. Life is out of focus, like a camera with fringed images slightly blurred.

⁓

Thus it was that the little girl in the yellow dress always watched carefully the behavior of her siblings and her parents, living as she did with a brother and a sister older by five and six years, two parents, and one great-aunt from the time she was three almost until she left home. You might say she did this for survival, rather than always believing what she was told.

71

Survival in her case consisted of avoiding being teased, reprimanded, lied to, or punished. She was a sensitive child and observed many things. She loved her sister when she read stories to her, but not when she yanked her hair because their mother had assigned her to shampoo it. Her big brother was her hero, except when he felt like tormenting her by punching her arm hard enough to leave a bruise. But the day he lay near the piano on the dining room floor and asked her to play again a portion of the Mozart sonata she was working on stayed in her memory forever.

"Of course you know we love you," her father might say, speaking sternly and criticizing her behavior. It didn't feel like love, though, and there was no later declaration of love to balance it with softness of tone or sincerity.

Another major theme of Friedman's work is the significance of anyone's family of origin for his or her functioning in other systems, like my involvement with music and performance. Writing about the dynamic of interaction in a family of origin, the author describes how one can carry this interaction forward into other processes across a lifetime. It's the family system as a *system* that matters. *Vis à vis* work systems as families, Friedman pointed out the following:

> *...even with a personal family, emotional process is passed down to new people who did not know the family members several "generations" back, and who were [not] around when processes now affecting the third, fourth, or even the fifth generation began.[4]*

Regarding the work of healing what needs to be healed in the brokenness of family pathos, Friedman issued a caveat:

> *It is not clear at all that knowledge of pathology is even necessary to promote healing.... One is always dealing with the diagnosed condition plus the family's own response to that condition.... Ultimately,*

healing and survival depend on existential categories: on vision, for example, on hope, on the imaginative capacity, on the ability to transcend the anxiety of those about us.[5]

I do not wish to portray my childhood as one filled with victimization by my family of origin. Indeed, some of the values I have described have contributed to my own determination to unravel my issues with music performance.

I have long since celebrated the positive legacy of values my family left to me, as well as a definite *joie de vivre* that was passed down from the very fabric of my mother's personality. Yet untangling the grossly constricting web of obstacles to my being free to flower in music performance—yes, even in comprehending music—has been healing beyond measure, healing what I only vaguely suspected needed to be healed. And beyond identifying a generational family condition (shame), understanding where my parents "were coming from," as we say today, has been an important key.

It would seem that we are all collections of parts of the particular family that bred us. Maybe we all belong to the same universal family that, separated, is wired to yearn to be reunited.

The "Aha!" Moment

Then, for our grown-up girl no longer a little girl in a yellow dress, an "Aha!" moment to put it all together.

The ground shifted under her spiritual feet as she discussed family matters with her friend and considered how children's problems sometimes stem from the troubles of those who came before. She thought they were talking about his children, but suddenly she was aware of her own relatives. In some mysterious and metaphoric way, the shame she had discovered in her father's life and her own deep anxiety about music at every level in her life came together. She was then quite sure that if her conversational friend, whom she had trusted profoundly for years, had not been a musician himself, the ingredients for the shift would have not been complete.

The new realization was like a little wet bird sitting on a limb, so fragile, so delicate, so not ready to fly. She knew this was a momentous discovery, but that's all she knew, and she wanted to let it sit still in her awareness, not subjecting itself to immediate analysis. She wanted to be in the experience, lest she fragment it before its meaning seeped into her consciousness.

As the little bird dried out, strengthened, and began to fly, the questions appeared: What was the connection between the family shame and her music making? Why did it not affect public speaking? Leadership? Responsibility? Courage in the face of adversity? Hard work? All of the values she had been taught and had absorbed for years? Skills that she had had occasion to practice? What was it about music? What had it always been about music that had kept her from playing the piano confidently?

Sometimes the real direction of our lives is not what we thought we were headed for at all. It's as if the driving force to accomplish or experience a certain thing is only a vehicle for something deeper. Thus it was that through her years of music training and then teaching, she had stumbled across a generational condition of shame that interfered with her musical development. When it was finally resolved and understood, it led her to a new freedom and blossoming that had never been there before.

To explore this change more fully, she returned to the letters in her closet. But before she could read them, they needed sorting. Among a large collection of all kinds of correspondence. written long before the days of email and easy use of long-distance phone, there were tomes written from her two siblings and herself to their parents, letters from her parents to their parents, and vice versa, courtship letters from her parents to each other and, poignantly, some seventy letters from her father's mother to her son, dating back more than ninety years. The process of sorting moved slowly but surely, and what she was to discover confirmed the earlier suspicions about her father's family.

Now she needed to connect the dots between family issues and her musical development.

That was the beginning of her understanding of The Shame, not to mention the confirmation of her mother's discomfort about the photograph albums.

After acknowledging that healthy shame means knowing our limitations and boundaries as humans (we are not omnipotent), John Bradshaw says healthy shame is "nourishing in that it moves us to seek new information and to learn new things."[6] It never allows us to believe we already know it all. The bulk of Bradshaw's work, though, is about the many aspects of toxic shame which, of course, is debilitating shame. One of the many sources of toxic shame is the family system, as noted before in the work of Edwin H. Friedman. Bradshaw puts it like this, speaking specifically of toxic shame.

> *The possibility of toxic shame begins with our source relationships. If our primary caregivers are shame based, they will act shameless and pass their toxic shame on to us…. Toxic shame is multigenerational. It is passed from one generation to the next.[7]*

It was at this point that I began to investigate the shame that Bradshaw had talked about and consider shame in my family of origin—the other side of healthy shame. When did one become the other?

Bradshaw says that toxic shame can take over one's identity, wherein one believes that this identity is flawed, that "…one is defective as a human being. Once shame is transformed into an identity, it becomes toxic and dehumanizing."[8] I knew I was getting closer to linking the family shame I carried with the anxiety I had felt about music performance for so many years.

In a brilliant presentation titled "Stage Fright: A Different Perspective" at the 2010 annual conference of the Music Teachers National Association (MTNA) , Frederic Chiu drew from the work of Donald Nathanson, author of *Shame and Pride*. Nathanson had expanded groundbreaking work by psychologist Sylvan S. Tomkins called "Affect Theory" (with emphasis on the first three letters—AFFect).

Affect Theory is a system of emotions and their physical manifestations. The nine affects and their manifestations are: Interest-Excitement, Enjoyment-Joy, Surprise-Startle, Distress-Anguish, Anger-Rage, Fear- Terror, Dissmell, Disgust, and Shame-Humiliation. The theory refers to both biological and psychological changes in a human being that occur when certain emotions arise. Nathanson, in fact, says that with the revelations of current brain research, the time has come to stop ignoring either field of study (biological or psychological) when talking about the other. Although it is not appropriate here to elaborate on the entire affect system discussed in the presentation, what interested me immediately was the affect *shame* and its extreme of *humiliation*. According to Chiu, the relationship of these two things is called, as are the other affects, "packages of body/mind/heart, inseparable."

In other words, when one feels shame (or any other of the nine affects), certain predictable bodily reactions can occur. For performers, these reactions (clammy hands, inability to think clearly, increased heart rate, shaking, heightened or extreme nervousness, etc.) can make a serious difference in the success of a performance. It is easy to see the relevance of Chiu's work to stage fright—everyone who experiences it will describe some of these physical symptoms.

Although many books and articles exist about managing the symptoms of stage fright, the works I have mentioned point to the value of understanding what happens to the emotions and the body under certain circumstances. Nathanson adds: "Affect is biology (physical); emotion is biography (personal history)." He describes shame as a family of negative emotions associated with incompetence, failure, and inadequacy—emotions that interfere with thinking:

> *Emotions, which are themselves events in the life of an individual, are triggered by events. Whatever resides in the memory is stored with its accompanying emotion; thus, each of us has a highly personal "information bank" of emotion-related data.*[9]

The Emerging Picture

In my musical experience as the little girl in the yellow dress, the well of emotion associated with piano performance was contaminated by shame that had been embedded disproportionately in my emotional makeup at various critical points in my development. Nathanson speaks of the affect of *interest* and its symptom, *excitement*, and concludes that when fulfillment of the event of interest is blocked, the intensity of this affect requires an intensity of shame–humiliation in equal proportion. As a protective mechanism, interest often wanes to reduce the shame–humiliation involved. In other words, lack of interest is a good way to avoid shame! (Could this be related to the number of adolescent middle school students who "lose interest" as their practice success drops off in the face of busy schedules?)

The affect program for shame–humiliation is triggered in these common situations when an impediment occurs and is painful in direct proportion to the degree of positive affect it limits (i.e., shame will occur whenever desire outruns fulfillment).

⌒

Our girl's experience in music performance was intense. Immersing herself in the sounds she played on the piano was important and gave her a great deal of pleasure. She cared intensely about communicating, or sharing, it.

In her beautiful net and taffeta floor-length dress, she ventured out on stage. Everything looked different. A sea of faces looked up at her, all anticipating what she would play at the piano. Somewhere deep inside, she would know that they were supportive, but what she felt was terror and fear of judgment. The stage lights were so bright that night that she couldn't see individual faces. In fact, she had never noticed how the lights reflected on the piano keys. There were shadows she hadn't seen before. "Träumerei" seemed remote. She wondered, "How am I ever going to remember how to play it?"

The recital turned out well in spite of her dread. She got through "Träumerei" without any problems. The terror subsided. Funny thing, though—when it was all over, the only thing she wanted was to go back onto the stage and play it again, for fun this time, when the frightening conditions were over and people weren't paying attention. She just wanted to hear and feel that wonderful grand piano.

⌒

In terms of music performance, Nathanson would say that shame interrupts effective communication between audience and performer, limiting the possibility of nonverbal intimacy and empathy in the flow of music. Shame outruns the desire to communicate.

It is one thing to read a scholarly treatise on the psychology of these emotions and quite another to recognize the patterns of a life's journey in anecdotal memories of it! I have certainly broadened my understanding of my own upbringing. My childhood years seem to me to have been during the period still influenced by customs and manners of nineteenth-century Europe, as well as the United States, as mentioned before.

I recently read Tolstoy's *Anna Karenina* for the first time. I found the characters' obsessions with propriety and proper behavior extremely disturbing to read. In the novel, communication between characters was difficult and obstructed by a lack of honesty and directness. The same can be found in almost any work of fiction written in the mid-nineteenth century. As much as I enjoy Jane Austen novels and period movies, my enjoyment is dampened by frustration for those poor folks who can't say what they mean for the possibility of shame descending on them.

My own memories of "proper" behavior included a ban on any expression of intense emotion, either positive or negative. Hyperbole and exaggeration were ridiculed. I was encouraged to be direct and truthful, but not about my feelings. By implication, at least to me, I should be critical of people who acted in plays and films because they were pretending, not behaving authentically. Yet we were regularly exposed to professionally performed drama and film. Perhaps I simply did not understand that acting was legitimate in those forms of literature.

"Don't 'emote' so!" was an admonition my parents hurled at my enthusiastic descriptions of events in my life. I was told often, "You take yourself too seriously!" Yet the family was intense, quarrelsome, and outspoken. In time, I pondered how a family in which the values of kindness toward others, truthfulness, and love of the world around us could be so unkind in its own interactions. The term "emotional intelligence," the title of a book by Daniel Goleman, came to mind as I began to understand that members of my family did not seem to have the skills to express their emotions honestly without sometimes being abusive, despite their high level of academic training.

It followed that intense expression in the form of music performance would be taboo. If "acting" were inauthentic as a behavior, then dramatic portrayal of musical ideas would be, too. In addition, anything calling attention to oneself was vain (bad) and was always considered to be a conscious manipulation of a given situation. Anything "fake" or manipulative was, in fact, reprehensible.

This book is about making the connections between my personal experience and the context of music performance. Even with the "Aha!" of understanding the family shame upon me, I hadn't quite realized that we are all composites of our family emotional histories. It's too obvious, of course. You have your father's ears, your uncle's big feet, your mother's hair, which thins terribly at an early age. Why not emotional components, too? Your temper, quick to flare up, like your grandfather's, your love of music like your grandmother's, mechanical acuity like your dad's. Or embedded shame from your father's side of the family tree.

The question haunting me through the years was why a lack of genuine self-confidence manifested itself in my relationship with music. What was it about music making that was different from other skills I had acquired?

I had identified shame as part of my emotional heritage. Was there something magical about the fabric of emotions woven through music in a unique way that I didn't understand quite yet?

V

Garden Walk

Perspective

Does Music Have Meaning?

To search for answers to my deepest questions, I looked for authors who have written about the meaning of music through the ages. Many writers and thinkers have pondered the power and meaning of music. Barbara Crowe, Director of Music Therapy at Arizona State University, says she wants to make the following points in her book, *Music and Soulmaking*:

> *Music is humankind's greatest joy and biggest mystery. This book is about music's ability to touch people in deep, profound ways.... [It will make] two basic points: first, that music is a powerful tool for healing and, second, that it is a source of human knowledge and understanding.... It is also about music's impact on the four levels of human functioning—mind, body, emotion, and spirit.[1]*

And Barry Green, in *The Mastery of Music*, says, "Passion and music have been deeply interwoven since a bird first sang to attract its mate, if not before."[2] Among his comments about passion as a zest for life is a discussion about passion for music itself, music making, playing music. He shares comments from performer/teacher Bonnie Hampton:

> *Music is a kind of expression that demands honesty. We all tend to wear masks of one kind or another in social situations—but when we play music, we have to make ourselves vulnerable, more open to each other as well as to the music.[3]*

Green himself expresses it eloquently:

> *Music touches feelings that words cannot. Music has the power to reach directly into the soul of everyone who participates in this experience. It is inspired by feelings and has the power to communicate the emotions better, perhaps, than any other form of communication. It is truly the international language that needs no translation.*[4]

Leonard B. Meyer, writing in *Emotion and Meaning in Music*, goes further. The significance of his writing for me is its affirmation that musical meaning may lie in the relationships of the sounds themselves, as well as in association of the sounds with cultural meanings based on what an individual listener has learned from his or her cultural base:

> *Composers and performers of all cultures, theorists of diverse schools and styles, aestheticians and critics of many different persuasions are all agreed that music has meaning and that this meaning is somehow communicated to both participants and listeners.*[5]

When all is said and done, though, the most inspiring statement about the meaning and function of music comes from Karl Paulnack's "Welcome Address" to incoming freshmen at The Boston Conservatory on February 21, 2009:

> *One of the first cultures to articulate how music really works were [sic] the ancient Greeks.... Astronomy was seen as the study of the relationships between observable, permanent, external objects, and music was seen as the study of relationships between invisible, internal, hidden objects. Music has a way of finding the big, invisible moving pieces inside our hearts and souls and helping us figure out the position of things inside us.*[6]

Paulnack gave many examples. One of the most profound is the musical composition "Quartet for the End of Time," by Olivier Messiaen, written from a Nazi prison camp in 1940. Puzzling about how anyone could write such music while imprisoned, here is what Paulnack surmised: "Art is part of survival; art is part of the human spirit, an unquenchable expression of who we are. Art is one of the ways in which we say, 'I am alive, and my life has meaning.'"

From these comments about musical meaning it is not hard to see that the honesty/vulnerability factor—one of those "big, invisible moving pieces"—is especially relevant to an understanding of why inherited family emotions attached themselves to music performance in my life. Musical expression through performance might reveal the vulnerable self filled with anxiety and shame. The self revealed would be just too much to bear, perhaps because its amorphous, immature form lacked the strength, or confidence, to take the risk.

Where Did Music Performance Come From?

Eventually, my larger questions pointed to larger contexts. Has stage fright always been present for musicians and other presenters and performers? Of course, I found this an impossible question to answer, but I did find some interesting ways to think about it.

Music performance was originally a community activity. In *Through Music to the Self,* Peter Michael Hamel recounts the function of music in ancient societies: "In all earlier world cultures, music stood at the service of ritual, of the holy cult, of consciousness expansion and the deepest in human experience."[7]

Hamel continues by quoting Carl Orff:

> *Elemental music is never just music. It is bound up with movement, dance, and speech, and so it is a form of music in which*

one must participate, in which one is involved not as a listener but as a co-performer.... Elemental music, word and movement, play, everything that awakens and develops the powers of the soul builds up the humus of the soul, the humus without which we face spiritual soil-erosion...[and] we face spiritual soil-erosion when man estranges himself from the elemental and loses his balance.[8]

A key word here is "co-performer." Community is central to communication, implied in the connection between soloist and audience.

Another example of performance for the community occurred in ancient China. The musician, highly trained in the scientific knowledge of how each note stood for something specific in the universe, was expected to compose music that expressed accordance with the celestial and world order. His role was tightly structured. He had been born and trained to it.

And on the other side of the world, records of instruments in rock art tell of the Puebloan peoples of the American Southwest. Ancient melodies played on indigenous materials that were made into musical instruments (conches, bones, wooden flutes), served to aid ceremonial healing. Amy Leinbach Marquis, archaeological researcher, describes the function of music in these early societies.:

Music wasn't just a form of entertainment to these people; it was their way of finding balance in the natural world. Since the Renaissance period, music has essentially become a spectator sport.... We sit down, fold our hands, listen, and clap politely. But to the ancient Puebloan, it was integral to their daily life and ceremony. It was like an extension of their language.[9]

So music was participatory. The participation culminated in a collective experience of community that included both performer(s) and listeners. We know that in similar collective experiences of making music, or playing it for the larger good, we experience belonging. We are part of a tribe.

Hamel reminds us that in early human cultures, certain rhythmic forms and melodic patterns grew up among the world's tribes and peoples and were passed down through generations as aural tradition. More than likely, the performers of this music derived the greatest pleasure from it, but this fact disturbed nobody, for everybody took part. There was no audience; there were no listeners.

~~~

The little girl in the yellow dress thoroughly enjoyed that early recital. Certainly she enjoyed praise and approval, although that wasn't what she remembered. She simply remembered how much fun it was to play the piano and how happy everyone seemed to be when she did that. But as she began to mature, she associated performance with the drama of formal concerts because attending them was, by this time, part of her experience. Delusions of grandeur were set in her desire for approval and acclaim, a recipe for shame and a continuous need for approval.

~~~

But maybe the sharing of one's accomplishment with another is somewhere between ego involvement, with its accompanying desire for approval, and simply playing or making music. William Westney cites this exquisite quote from J.M. Thorburn: "All the genuine, deep delight of life is in showing people the mud-pies you have made; and life is at its best when we confidingly recommend our mud-pies to each other's sympathetic consideration."[10]

As a teacher, I participated in many student events outside the studio and held regular traditional studio recitals. When we were ready for a recital, the students and I consistently stressed having a good time playing in these events and talked about how far we had progressed in the learning of a special piece, whatever the outcome on the performance day might be.

Apart from sharing the "mud pies," I often wondered if it were possible to reach excellence in performance without the goals of performing events.

In today's American culture, I wasn't sure. I never liked competitions and only cautiously suggested participating in them with certain students. It seemed to me that it was a distraction to associate performing music with winning or losing.

From my own experience and from many conversations with colleagues, I know that competing can motivate students to work hard and aim for superior achievement. What kind of inner motivation to push ourselves to superb achievement is needed? Can we do something exceedingly well just because the doing is possible? ("Climb the mountain because it is there?") Can young students "master" a piece without the goal of a recital performance or competitive event, after which they will receive an award accompanied by enthusiastic praise and approval? Can maturing students be thrilled by music they are playing simply because they are caught up in its beauty and because they have been able to release its "magic" through their abilities? Once again I am reminded of the vitality and spontaneous sharing of young children that sometimes get aborted as they grow older.

A Shift in Function

Music performance evolved toward entertainment—from the communal experience to the entertainment of an audience, creating a separation between performer and listener. Most people will reply, when asked why we have music, that we need it for our own enjoyment, that "music exists for relaxation, for aesthetic enjoyment, for relieving boredom, for spiritual uplift, for passing the time, for edification."[11]

As far as enjoyment is concerned, almost any independent piano teacher today will affirm that most parents, thinking they have only two choices for their young students, will say, "I just want her to have fun. She doesn't have to be a concert pianist," usually unaware that hard work and commitment lead to the expertise that makes a profound sort of fun possible, and that becoming a concert pianist is an unlikely possibility anyway! The hard work is about building the foundation that offers the *freedom* to have fun. It should include analyzing and memorizing at least part of student repertoire, strictly for growth and enjoyment, not to mention the sheer fun of "owning" a piece of music with the freedom that memorizing can bring. Productive practice will lead to memorizing almost automatically. Naturally, this hard work includes the not-always-fun routine exercises that literally train the physical aspects of playing instruments.

Not so long ago, in the mid-eighteenth century, music was still the "faithful servant of theology" in Europe. Around the middle of the century, though, things began to change. Nowhere is this shift in the function of music in our Western heritage better described than in the delightful book *Evening in the Palace of Reason* by James R. Gaines, subtitled *Bach Meets Frederick the Great in the Age of Enlightenment.*

Written almost in novel form, this is the story of how Bach's traditional view that music is to serve spiritual purposes (even to the extent that certain configurations of melody represented certain spiritual states of being) clashed with coming changes. Bach was strongly influenced by the great theologian Martin Luther (1483–1546), leader of the Protestant Reformation.

King Frederick, on the other hand, was all for music's providing pleasure, both to play in ensemble and to listen to, much more as an end in itself, still in community, but without the overlay of spiritual meaning.

The goal of the Baroque composer generally was to move the listener in a certain direction, which reinforced his notion of himself as an artisan, not as an artist expressing an idea or feeling of his own but as a professional with an assigned task and particular "teachable" ways of doing it. It was assumed that melodic figures and harmonies could encode spiritual meanings and were intended to elicit specific positive or negative messages. These messages were called "Affections." It was not necessary for the performers or listeners to be aware of these intentions for them to be effective.

Gaines tells us that scholars had already described Affections as a limited number of moods: wonder, love, hatred, desire, joy, and sadness. In fact, one frequently understood motto was "Music is nothing other than the knowledge of the order of all things."[12]

The Birth of the Artist

As the function of music began to change in the West, or at least broaden, the performer serving the community evolved into the performer as the embodiment of individual expression—as artist. Audiences became more interested in being entertained by the performer's own personal interpretation of someone else's composition or even of his own music. And the solo artist worked slavishly to perfect the score of a great composer, work done largely in isolation, and present his or her accomplishment.

The musician previously had been a regular member of the "tribe," or ritually identified group, as simply a contributor to the collective experience. It was natural, then, for the musician to experience stepping apart from the tribe or society as he moved toward individual presentation as entertainment. No matter how modern we are, even today, stepping away from family traditions or local customs can threaten the status quo, for the family or clan is the modern tribe.

The dynamic of doing *anything* at all to prevent change, or to maintain this status quo, is then activated. And when an individual steps out of the expectations of the tribe, he calls attention to himself. This sort of "spotlighting" can threaten the well-being of the community by fostering jealousy, criticism, competition, and conflict. It can then be followed by an emerging hierarchy, class distinction, and anxiety. It may be seen as an individual saying, "Look at me. I am special."

The deviation from the ancient value of participation, wherein the group experience in music was part of the community's identity, exacted a price. The performer was now isolated, ostracized, because his or her expression of self set this very self apart from the tribe. This is not to say that specialization, requiring many hours of work honing a craft, is necessarily against tribal values. The approval of the tribe, however, might be a critical factor in the tribe's support of this isolated work.

Or, to put it another way, when the musician—or any other solo component of the ritual function of community—became a soloist for the entertainment of the tribe, he or she moved apart, separating from the group and standing in a different position altogether. The nature of "tribe" is that anyone who moves outside and goes in his or her own direction, especially if it is different, stands to be ostracized by the home group by becoming "other." Herein lies the potential for shame and its companions: anxiety and fear.

Ostracism

What happens when we are ostracized, or cast out? In a scholarly book called *Ostracism—the Power of Silence*, Kipling D. Williams looks at ostracism and its effects with experiments that highlight its targets, or victims, as well as its perpetrators:

> *Individuals who deviate from others' expectations are often the targets of ostracism. Consequently, it appears as though the primary function of ostracism is to bring the target back into the fold or to expel him or her altogether. Either outcome strengthens the ostracizing group's cohesiveness...the simple act of being ignored [ostracized]*

simultaneously attacks...fundamental human needs. Our sense of connection and belonging is severed; the control or desire between our actions and outcomes is uncoupled; our self-esteem is shaken by feelings of shame, guilt, or inferiority.[13]

The soloist stands alone. Where is the meeting of the exacting, difficult, often thrilling work to reach a point of mastery and the spiritual possibility in the content of the music? Will the performance be an occasion in which all is transcended, the performer and audience become one, the awareness of the performing artist's self is overcome, and genuine communication takes place in moments that seem magical?

I believe that the deepest roots of performance anxiety, quite beyond anyone's personal history, may well lie in the shift from community performance to solo presentation.

VI

Harvest

Epilogue

Communication

Everyone knows that the ability to communicate is a basic human need. Karl Paulnack said it another way in the Boston Conservatory speech:

> *Music is a basic need of human survival. Music is one of the ways we make sense of our lives, one of the ways in which we express feelings when we have no words, a way for us to understand things with our hearts when we can't with our minds.... Music can slip beneath our conscious reality to get at what's really going on inside us the way a good therapist does.*[1]

Is there a difference, or a separation, between "serious" music and "popular" music? If there is, then Paulnack and others quoted here are talking about the former. In fact, returning in a way to music's most profound function, he says this in the same speech to the freshmen:

> *You're not here to become an entertainer, and you don't have to sell yourself. The truth is you don't have anything to sell; being a musician isn't about dispensing a product, like selling used cars. I'm not an entertainer.... You're here to become a sort of therapist for the human soul....*

Certainly a kind of community has continued through time with group performance. Collaborative classical performing in quartets, trios, duos, and orchestras has always been there. A sense of community has usually developed, at least among the group of performers, who have, in their diligent practice, made music together. In a chapter called "A Drama of Relationships," Christopher Small says this:

> *The type of dramatic orchestral work that emerged around 1750 was initially strictly for entertainment and was intended as introduction to, or diversion from, the more serious business of the occasion at which it was played [opera, theatre, Mass, etc.].... The intention was to create something graceful, elegant, and above all, entertaining.*[2]

What, then, do we do with the type of mass communication that takes place, as we all know, with teeming audiences at rock concerts responding by yelling, singing, waving arms, whistling, and clapping wildly? What are the rites inherent in these performances? Do rock stars provide communal ritual for a society whose members are encouraged to be "individuals" and yet feel alienated from the whole? Are these concerts first and foremost entertainment? Is this a combination of ritual and entertainment? No matter what the answers are to these questions, the focus of the event is still on the stars, the performers, and what they can do for the crowds.

What I have been more narrowly concerned with here is the traditionally trained piano student who signs up for lessons that require isolated practice to develop high skill and whose presentation of his or her new skill is most likely to be a solo performance for an audience of listeners. It's still about the self and what the self can produce for the pleasure of others. We would hope that sometimes, at least, the presentation, or performance, becomes more important than the spotlight on the individual. Everyone forgets who it is and how he or she is doing at the recital and is caught up in the music itself.

In the studio, we spoke of this as "magic."

Letting Go

Taking a long look back after teaching for forty-five years, the now-retired teacher could say she had really loved teaching piano and remembered many special moments with students as they explored music together. She encountered the same problems as other teachers of motivating students. Nevertheless, there were joyful and fulfilling days in abundance.

She became more and more at ease playing in public and performing solos from memory in a local performance group of teachers. As the studio matured and some students moved into advanced work, there were many opportunities for her to play second piano with orchestral reductions to piano concerti, other accompanying parts, duos, and quartets. She branched out through professional volunteer work in teachers' organizations and through presenting programs and workshops for colleagues, another source of fulfillment as well as a stimulating challenge. Even in retirement, she continued many of these activities and had the pleasure of being an adjudicator, or listener, in many festivals each year.

The time came to leave the world of performance anxiety behind. Playing Brahms in a recital in her new location was a wonderful experience. Butterflies, but not dragons, were peacefully present—no, not so peaceful—rather, fluttering with excitement! The setting was an art gallery, and the occasion a "fireside concert." In the glow of the artistically lit setting, she felt happy and fulfilled. Afterward, she marveled at the change that had seeped slowly through her.

Her relationship to the piano was somehow new. She didn't need to perform in a formal setting anymore; she needed only to explore and share the lifelong yearning to make music without the overlay of feeling somehow inadequate, like an imposter.

So it was that understanding my family's legacy, studying humanities, which so enriched my life, helping students learn to play the piano and appreciate music, and learning a little about traditions of music performance led me from dissonance to resolution.

As if from a hilltop nearby, I could see the path of my journey through the garden. The whole scene was full of the blossoms of discovery, the weeds of thwarted accomplishment rooted out and tossed away.

Fini

NOTES

Preface

[1] Jean Houston, *Jump Time* (New York: Dell Publishing Co, Inc., 1980) 109.

I. Seeds Sown in Uncertain Ground

[1] Stewart Gordon, *Etudes for Piano Teachers* (Oxford: Oxford University Press,1995) 143.

[2] William Westney, *The Perfect Wrong Note, Learning to Trust Your Musical Self* (Pompton Plains, New Jersey: Amadeus Press, 2003) 29.

[3] Alice Miller *The Drama of the Gifted Child* (New York: Basic Books, Inc., 1981) 11.

[4] Nancy O'Neill Breth, *Practicing the Piano* (Milwaukee: Hal Leonard Corporation, 2012)

[5] Daniel Coyle, *The Talent Code* (New York: Bantam Dell (Random House, Inc., 2009) 43–44.

[6] William Westney, *The Perfect Wrong Note, Learning to Trust Your Musical Self* (Pompton Plains, New Jersey: Amadeus Press, 2003) 61–62.

[7] Malcolm Gladwell, *Outliers* (New York: Little, Brown and Company, 2008)

II. Buds and Weeds

[1] Sally Bonkrude, *Conscious Performing...from fear to freedom!* (Wheat Ridge, Colorado: Inner Source Publishing, 2008) xi-xii.

IV. Taproot

1 John Bradshaw, *Healing the Shame That Binds You* (Deerfield Beach, Florida: Health Communications, Inc,. 1988). vii.

2 Edwin H. Friedman *Generation to Generation* (New York: The Guilford Press, 1985) 31–32.

3 Susan Griffin *Wrestling with the Angel of Democracy* (Boston: Trumpeter Books, 2008) 90.

4 Edwin H. Friedman *Generation to Generation* (New York: The Guilford Press, 1985) 198.

5 Edwin H. Friedman *Generation to Generation* (New York: The Guilford Press, 1985) 5.

6 John Bradshaw, *Healing the Shame That Binds You* (Deerfield Beach, Florida: Health Communications, Inc. 1988). 9.

7 John Bradshaw, *Healing the Shame That Binds You* (Deerfield Beach, Florida: Health Communications, Inc. 1988) 25.

8 John Bradshaw, *Healing the Shame That Binds You* (Deerfield Beach, Florida: Health Communications, Inc. 1988) vii

9 Donald L. Nathanson, *Shame and Pride, Affect, Sex, and the Birth of the Self* (New York: W.W. Norton & Company, 1992) 48.

V. Garden Walk

1 Barbara Crowe, *Music and Soul Making, Toward a New Theory of Music Therapy* (Lanham, Maryland: Scarecrow Press, Inc., 2004) xi.

2 Barry Green, *The Mastery of Music* (New York: Broadway Books, a Division of Random House, Inc., 2003) 117.

3 Barry Green, *The Mastery of Music* (New York: Broadway Books, a Division of Random House, Inc., 2003) 121.

4 Barry Green, *The Mastery of Music* (New York: Broadway Books, a Division of Random House, Inc., 2003) 122.

5 Leonard B. Meyer, *Emotion and Meaning in Music* (Chicago: University of Chicago Press, 1956) 1.

6 Karl Paulnack, "Welcome Address to Incoming Freshmen," (Boston: The Boston Conservatory, February 21, 2009)

[7] Peter Michael Hamel, *Through Music to the Self* (Munich: Element Books, 1976) 7.

[8] Peter Michael Hamel, *Through Music to the Self* (Munich: Element Books, 1976). 18.

[9] Amy Leinbach Marquis, "Ancient Melodies," *National Parks Magazine* (Washington, D.C., Summer 2010) 28–29.

[10] William Westney *The Perfect Wrong Note, Learning to Trust Your Musical Self* (Pompton Plains, New Jersey: Amadeus Press, 2003) 27.

[11] Peter Michael Hamel, *Through Music to the Self* (Munich: Element Books, 1976). 7.

[12] James R. Gaines *Evening in the Palace of Reason, Bach Meets Frederick the Great in the Age of Enlightenment,* (New York: Harper Perennial, 2005). 83–84.

[13] Kipling D. Williams, *Ostracism-The Power of Silence* (New York: The Guilford Press, 2001). 11.

VI. Harvest

[1] Karl Paulnack "Welcome Address to Incoming Freshmen," (Boston: The Boston Conservatory, February 21, 2009).

[2] Christopher Small, *Musicking, the Meanings of Performing and Listening* (Middletown, Connecticut: Wesleyan University Press, 1998). 158.

BIBLIOGRAPHY

Works Cited

Bonkrude, Sally. *Conscious Performing...from fear to freedom!* Wheat Ridge, Colorado: Inner Source Publishing, 2008.

Bradshaw, John. *Healing the Shame That Binds You.* Deerfield Beach, Florida: Health Communications, Inc., 1988.

Breth, Nancy O'Neill. *Practicing the Piano.* Milwaukee, Wisconsin: Hal Leonard Corporation, 2012.

Chiu, Frederic, "Stage Fright: A Different Perspective" (paper presented at MTNA Conference, Albuquerque, New Mexico, March 21–24, 2010).

Coyle, Daniel. *The Talent Code.* New York: Bantam Dell (Random House, Inc.), 2009.

Crowe, Barbara. *Music and Soul Making: Toward a New Theory of Music Therapy.* Lanham, Maryland: Scarecrow Press, Inc., 2004.

Friedman, Edwin H. *Generation to Generation.* New York: The Guilford Press, 1985.

Gaines, James R. *Evening in the Palace of Reason: Bach Meets Frederick the Great in the Age of Enlightenment.* New York: Harper Perennial, 2005.

Gladwell, Malcolm. *Outliers.* New York: Little, Brown & Company, 2008.

Gordon, Stewart. *Etudes for Piano Teachers.* Oxford: Oxford University Press, 1995.

Green, Barry. *The Mastery of Music.* New York: Broadway Books, a division of Random House, Inc., 2003.

Griffin, Susan. *Wrestling with the Angel of Democracy: On Being an American Citizen.* Boston: Trumpeter Books, 2008.

Hamel, Peter Michael. *Through Music to the Self.* Munich: Element Books, 1976.

Houston, Jean. *Jump Time.* Boulder, Colorado: Sentient Publications, 2004.

Marquis, Amy Leinbach. "Ancient Melodies," *National Parks Magazine,* Washington, DC: National Parks Conservation Association, 2010.

Meyer, Leonard B. *Emotion and Meaning in Music.* Chicago: University of Chicago Press, 1956.

Miller, Alice. *The Drama of the Gifted Child.* English Translation. New York. Basic Books, Inc., 1981.

Nathanson, Donald L. *Shame and Pride, Affect, Sex, and the Birth of the Self.* New York: W. W. Norton & Company, 1992.

Paulnack, Karl. *Welcome Address.* Boston: The Boston Conservatory, 2009.

Small, Christopher. *Musicking: The Meanings of Performing and Listening.* Middletown, Connecticut: Wesleyan University Press, 1998.

Thurman, Judith. *Isak Dinesen: The Life of a Storyteller.* New York: St. Martin's Press, 1982.

Westney, William. *The Perfect Wrong Note.* Pompton Plains, New Jersey: Amadeus Press, 2003.

Williams, Kipling D. *Ostracism—The Power of Silence.* New York: The Guilford Press, 2001.

Further Reading

Apel, Willi. *Harvard Dictionary of Music*, Second Edition. Cambridge, MA: Harvard University Press, 1970.

Cutting, Linda Katherine. *Memory Slips: A Memoir of Music and Healing.* New York: Harper Perennial, 1997.

Gardner, Howard. *Art, Mind, & Brain: A Cognitive Approach to Creativity.* Cambridge, Massachusetts: Basic Books, 1982.

Goleman, Daniel. *Emotional Intelligence.* New York: Bantam Books, 1995.

Houston, Jean. *Life Force: The Psycho-Historical Recovery of the Self.* New York: Dell Publishing Co., Inc., 1980.

Houston, Jean. *The Search for the Beloved.* New York: G. P. Putnam's Sons, 1987.

Jensen, Robert. *All My Bones Shake: Seeking a Progressive Path to the Prophetic Voice.* Brooklyn, New York: Soft Skull Press, 2009.

Jourdain, Robert. *Music, the Brain, and Ecstasy.* New York: Harper Collins, 1997.

Klingenstein, Beth Gigante. *The Independent Piano Teacher's Studio Handbook.* Milwaukee, Wisconsin. Hal Leonard Corporation, 2009.

Langer, Suzanne K. *Philosophy in a New Key.* Cambridge, Massachusetts. Harvard University Press, 1942.

Lefrancois, Guy R. *Psychology for Teaching.* 10th Edition. Belmont, California: Wadsworth/Thomson Learning, 2000.

Maslow, Abraham H. *The Farther Reaches of Human Nature.* New York. Viking Press, 1971.

May, Rollo. *Love and Will,* New York. Dell Publishing Co., Inc., 1969.

Music, Diane Dalton. *Songs That We Sang Together: The Life and Death of an American Family.* Vols. I, II, III. Kearney, Nebraska: Morris Publishing, 1999.

Pillay, Srinivasan S. *Life Unlocked.* New York: Rodale, Inc., 2010.

Ristad, Eloise. *A Soprano on Her Head.* Moab, Utah: Real People Press, 1982.

Samples, Bob. *The Metaphoric Mind: A Celebration of Creative Consciousness.* Reading, Massachusetts: Addison–Wesley Publishing Company, 1976.

Storr, Anthony. *Music and the Mind.* New York: The Free Press, a Division of Macmillan, Inc., 1992.

Tame, David. *The Secret Power of Music.* Rochester, VT: Destiny Books, 1984.

Tolstoy, Leo. *Anna Karenina.* Constance Garnett, tr. New York: Doubleday & Company, Inc., 1948.

12121239R10075

Made in the USA
San Bernardino, CA
09 June 2014